*Will,*
*I hope*
*good friend ... will be ok!*
*Some help, if and when you travel*
*Down the deer hunting path*
*Best wishes*
*Bb*

# Back Yard
# Whitetail Hunter

## A Beginner's Guide

## To Whitetail Hunting Close To Home

## by

## Joseph Grifoni Jr.

*Hey Will!*
*Best wishes next season.*

# Xulon
## PRESS

Copyright © 2013 by Joseph Grifoni Jr.

*Back Yard Whitetail Hunter*
*A Beginner's Guide To Whitetail Hunting Close To Home*
by Joseph Grifoni Jr.

Printed in the United States of America

ISBN 9781625098320

All rights reserved solely by the author. The author guarantees all contents are original and do not infringe upon the legal rights of any other person or work. No part of this book may be reproduced in any form without the permission of the author. The views expressed in this book are not necessarily those of the publisher.

Unless otherwise indicated, Bible quotations are taken from the New International Version. Copyright © 1973, 1978, 1984 by Zondervan Corporation.

Edited by Linda A. Libert. Linda is a manuscript editor, ghostwriter and proofreader. She is also a professional speaker, teacher, private tutor & blogger (http://www.hearttohearttalks.com/Blog/)

www.xulonpress.com

# Dedication

*T*his work is dedicated to my Lord and Savior, Jesus Christ, who from His infinite mind and loving heart imagined the magnificent whitetail deer and then created it from nothing. It is a humbling and great truth to know that He gave us everything in this world to offer back to Him in glory.

I further dedicate this work to my wife Carolyn, and my children Lauren and Peter. Each of my family members supports me in my efforts to fill our freezer with wild game meats. Carolyn has invariably pushed me to success when I didn't have enough faith in my abilities or when I was hesitant to spend money or time on my favorite hobby. Carolyn is empathetic both when I fail and when I succeed. She is 1 Corinthians 12:26 in action! Being a fabulous cook, she is continuously experimenting with new recipes and preparing old favorites. Her heart is like an orchard at harvest time! There have been occasions when I have rolled over in bed to turn off my alarm clock that was ringing well over an hour before first light.

As I began drifting back to sleep, Carolyn would put both of her feet on my back and push me out of bed with a cute comment such as "You can't get one from here."

Lauren, from a very young age, would smile from ear to ear and get into all my photos with my fresh kills. Aspiring to be a veterinarian, she has dissected a few deer hearts. Peter encourages me in another way. Nobody is happier with the smell of a grill full of marinated steaks! Peter also shares a desire for the woods. When left to his own, he grabs a toy gun and treks into his little piece of wilderness to battle imaginary enemies and set up camps so he can live off of the land. Carolyn, Lauren, Peter, you are all an indescribable blessing to me.

I would like to thank those who have made a personal investment in my life. Thank you, Mom and Dad. Although you may not always understand my passions, you always love me. Thank you, Les Harriman (Uncle Les), for generously sharing your hunting talents when I need them. Thank you, Al Dunfee, for your example of dedication to family first and then the hunt, and for encouraging me to pursue this project. Thank you, Chuck Andon. From the first time I picked up a bow, you respected my desire to learn to hunt and never laughed when I was completely clueless. Special thanks to my editor and patient friend Linda Libert. Your wordsmithing not only turned my writing into proper English but you clarified the entire message. And to the most doting grandfather I have ever met, Bob Nesland. You are an authentic Christian man who has led his family through two generations. Yet you still manage to find time to hunt, fish and lead boy scout troops in the Alaskan Wilderness. I hope to one day be a man with a heart as powerful as yours!

Finally, I dedicate this work to you, the reader. I hope you are the one who will carry the great hunting traditions to the field. Then I hope you pass them down to generations to come. Best wishes!

# Foreword

Robert Nesland

*I*t's very pleasing when you meet someone who is exceptional at what he does. It's even more pleasing when that person is a good friend. There are hidden talents in Joe Grifoni that delight and amaze, such as writing a book—a really great book—full of information and stories that are fun to read.

There's a lack of knowledge about how to observe wildlife, or distinguish one track from another. This is why Joe's book is both timely and important. His knowledge of deer hunting and his step-by-step tutorial on how to identify all the different animals in your woods are wonderful.

I recently took my granddaughters to Story Land, an amusement park for children, and there was a sign in front of a water ride that said: "If you go on this ride you <u>will</u> get wet!" I confidently say that if you hunt the way Joe teaches you to, you <u>will</u> get your deer.

Years ago I was deer hunting in PA. There were about eight or nine of us who had hunted together for over 20 years and knew the land and the deer herds well. We were putting on a drive, a way of flushing out deer, with three drivers and five shooters. Three of the shooters, myself included, were on the edge of a woods road facing a fairly open area that had been clear cut five years earlier, leaving only small bushes and trees. When hunters drive deer, the buck will often sneak out one way sending the does running as a herd the other way as a diversion. Over the years of hunting this area we shot many does, but never a buck. Almost an hour passed with all of us watching intently for the deer to be pushed into our area, when suddenly a large buck jumped up from the ground 20 feet in front of us. He bounded over the road and was gone. To this day it's still called Magic Valley, but there was nothing magic about it. That buck had seen us moving about or picked up an unfamiliar smell, and crept on his belly keeping all three of us in sight. I doubt if Special Forces could have done better; it's a lesson Joe teaches in his book—one I learned the hard way by losing a chance to take a fine buck.

The beauty of Joe's book is that he prepares you to be ready to take advantage of every opportunity to be successful.

Today with more and more families leaving rural areas and moving to urban places it's much more complicated to organize a hunt. Years ago when I lived in PA, I could take my rifle and walk out my back door to hunt thousands of acres of state forest. My friends and I and our children hunted a four hundred acre parcel ten minutes from our homes. Schools in PA were closed on opening day of deer season, the first Monday after Thanksgiving. Young boys of ages 12 and 13 would stack their shotguns inside the door of the bake shop while they ate their donuts on their way home from hunting. Those days are almost gone and a lot of the knowledge is no longer being passed on; that's why Joe's book is so very important. It is chock full of all the information you will ever need to be a successful hunter or observer of wildlife.

If I could give my grandson only one book on hunting it would be this one. . .

## Back Yard Whitetail Hunter
### A Beginner's Guide
### To Whitetail Hunting Close To Home

# Introduction

*L*ike many boys I developed an interest in hunting at a very young age. The interest may have come from reading stories about the early settlers of this country. My father was not a hunter. None of my uncles or adult friends hunted either. Lacking someone to teach me, I put my dream of heading to the woods in pursuit of wild game on hold. After college I got married and eventually built a home in a quiet rural neighborhood. On occasion I saw deer and other wildlife on my property and in adjacent woodlands. I responded to wildlife sightings back then as I probably will for the rest of my life—with awe. I am especially awed by the sight of whitetail deer. During the first autumn after we moved into our new home, I awoke one morning to the sound of gunfire. The realization that a few of the "locals" were hunting the patchwork of forests in the town exhilarated me. Then it occurred to me that I didn't need to drive to a camp in the wilderness to hunt. I could do it in my home town! This epiphany spurred me to get involved immediately. For my birthday I purchased a bow and began to practice shooting it in my backyard. My shelves filled with books on animal tracks, and I subscribed to sportsman's magazines. Interestingly the few hunters I came to know were business people with limited recreational time. Although I longed for someone to teach me how to become a successful hunter, none of these folks could spare the hours it would take for sufficient instruction. After many years of personal effort and one class in tracking, I can say I am primarily self-taught. Although this type of learning is slow and is fraught with trial and error, I can honestly say it worked out well for me. Through personal experience I have gained a body of knowledge that is truly effective. The self-instruction process has been (mostly) a pleasure, and I expect to enjoy learning more every season.

Very likely you have heard people's reasons for why they enjoy deer hunting. They may have been eager to describe its benefits, especially about how a well-regulated hunt will keep the herds, packs, flocks and gaggles healthy by maintaining populations that can be supported by the land. (The scientific data support this claim.) Some folks will bring up human health issues and state that deer transport ticks that can carry Lyme disease. Animal and automobile collisions are reduced by managing populations as well. Some less noble reasons are also raised, such as "They are eating my shrubs!" But honestly, none of those reasons, as valid as they are, drive me into the woods to hunt. I will confess to you right now that when my alarm clock rings an hour before sunrise, I am not thinking about saving the bushes, stopping automobile collisions or even helping to stop the spread of disease! These reasons, in support of hunting, are indeed great byproducts of the tradition. However, I think an honest and far greater answer to why we hunt is "because it's thrilling!" I believe this answer is the same for the majority of hunters.

Few activities in my life give me the thrills that whitetail hunting can offer. I can barely describe the joy and freedom that fills me when I walk into a crisp autumn or winter forest with a bow in my hand or a gun on my shoulder. The forest calls to me. I believe the same is true for anyone who is passionate about what he does. It is much like how the sea calls the sailor, and only the sailor hears it. He finds the call irresistible, so he goes. Many will look at him and not understand why he must answer the call because they do not hear it. I am not a sailor so I don't hear the call of the sea. But I understand it. The sailor hears the call of the sea because the very nature of the sea is within him. Much like the call of the sea, there is a call to the hunt. I hear it because the nature of the hunt is within me.

When we see the painter, the ballet dancer or the musician perform, we get an idea of what they experience when they indulge their hearts and do what they are called to do. We can see the joy they have when they perform. We can see the result of their artistry and the beauty of their talents. I believe this is true for anyone who does what he enjoys and is willing to work hard at it. I will never understand exactly how a dancer feels when performing because I am not a dancer. But if I look with my heart, I can see a person who is doing what she is made to do. I can see the beauty in it and rejoice with her.

Much like the sailor, the hunter's art is not often put on display for the world to see. Certainly a large part of it is found in the freezer full of wild meat. Family and friends gather gratefully around the table for dinner. Oh to sit together and enjoy a healthy and wonderful meal! And if I am asked, I will relish telling the story of how that animal came to be ours.

The forest is a unique setting for fellowship and teamwork through which strong bonds are formed. I've followed dogs and tromped through fields trying to scare up pheasants with great guys. And I have tracked deer through the swamps in the dark of night with dedicated friends. It makes my heart glad to be with these people. And to see my kiddos squirrel hunting around the local woodlands delights me as well. Who knows? Maybe they will hear the call of the whitetail hunt as they get older. They too will have the opportunity to observe natural wonders such as a fisher cat tearing up a log in pursuit of a squirrel, coyotes howling to each other, and young bucks rattling their antlers.

Through stories, you will come to know the wide variety of emotions that hunting brings out of me. My wife jokes that I am crazed from mid-July to the beginning of deer season, full of anticipation! At the beginning of every season, and especially during the first few hunts, I get butterflies in my stomach. I feel edgy, as though I am on the bench of a playoff game knowing that the coach is getting ready to put me in! Although I do not consider myself a very emotional guy, hunting moves my heart through a wide spectrum of emotions. I think that the object of a man's passions will bring out such feelings. Throughout a full day's hunt I experience a full spectrum of moods that range from a great sense of anticipation to boredom to intense pressure to perform and ultimately to joy and contentment. There are other hunts that have included disappointment and heartbreak, but those are rare.

I live in the middle of Essex County, Massachusetts. Aside from a few Wildlife Management Areas (WMAs) ranging in size from 1000 to 5000 acres, the majority of local deer hunting takes place in rural suburban woodlands. When my wife and I moved to town in 1993, our neighborhood was clearly rural. But as the years have passed, it seems that "suburban" is becoming a better description for our home town. Hunting on these lands pre-dates human record-keeping and still occurs today. The forests and thickets are home to one of my favorite quarries, the whitetail deer.

I hope to whet your appetite for the whitetail hunt. If you already have the interest then I hope to help you succeed by sharing what I have learned. Find a nice shade tree or a hammock. Or if the season is cold, find a wood stove and a couch with a view into the yard. I think you will enjoy this. Oh, and if you have a birthday coming up, ask for a game freezer!

There are a plethora of videos available that teach hunting skills and tactics. They are great for the beginner and there are a few nuggets in there even for the advanced hunter. Generally these videos are shot in large expanses of wilderness or large farm lands surrounded by forest. If that is where you intend to hunt, they are perfect. For the suburban or backyard whitetail hunter, there is still a bit of information that can be gleaned from these videos. Don't hesitate to study them. But, it has been my experience that some of the tactics used in these videos do not work well in suburban areas. For example: One well respected group of hunters encourage driving along logging roads in a truck in snow covered woods in search of a deer track of the size animal that they would like to shoot. Then while keeping awareness high and advancing along the track on foot, the hunter is encouraged to follow the deer for great distances until the deer is located and shot. That is great! However, if you try that in a suburban area, you will find yourself being forced to walk through people's yards or land posted "No Hunting". Or you might cross major roads or even enter areas where possession of a firearm might raise eyebrows or be illegal. So, that will be frustrating. In suburbia, this technique will at best push a deer to another hunter. He will be happy to shoot, tag and drag the deer home without even offering you a "thank you" because he never even knew you were involved.

Hunting the deep wilderness and the small patches of forests near civilization have more similarities than differences. The essentials for these conditions will be addressed with added attention given to the back yard whitetail hunting scenario. It is for this style of hunting that I want you to be especially prepared for!

# Preface

*A*s you read this book, please consider the concept below. It is my hope that as you enter the hunting experience, the natural world will declare it to you. For many, this concept will sound contrary to the ideas that are so prevalent in the world today, but it flows with sincerity from my personal convictions:

Wildlife conservation that creates sanctuaries for plants and animals is a philosophy of separation, not connection. It is unnatural for man simply to observe nature and leave it untouched. Because he is made in the image of God he is not the enemy of nature. Mankind is here to exercise wise stewardship of the Earth and all of its resources. It is his calling to work the Earth and harvest its bounty. The philosophy of separation can generate a fear of harming the natural world that reduces man to being a mere observer. This "hands off" status benefits neither man nor nature.

*"The fear and dread of you will fall on all the beasts of the earth, and on all the birds in the sky, on every creature that moves along the ground, and on all the fish in the sea; they are given into your*

*hands. Everything that lives and moves about will be food for you. Just as I gave you the green plants, I now give you everything."*
Genesis 9:2,3

# Contents

Dedication ........................................................................ v

Foreword by Robert Nesland ........................................ ix

Introduction ................................................................ xiii

Preface ......................................................................... xxi

Chapter 1: Get Out Of Your Arm Chair!

(The Wilderness Outside Your Door) ...................... 27

Chapter 2: Deer Don't Fly! (Deer Sign) ..................... 34

Chapter 3: WOW, What A Big Brain.

(Deer And Human Abilities) .................................. 63

Chapter 4: Hiding In The Open (Introducing

the Four Dimensions Of Camouflage

And How To Beat The Amazing Deer Senses) ........ 79

Chapter 5: Oh My Gosh! You STINK!

(Scent Control) ...................................................... 86

Chapter 6: James Bond Or Maxwell Smart?

(How To Camouflage Your

Movement) ........................................................... 107

Chapter 7: Elmer Fudd

(What To Do With Sound) .................................... 121

Chapter 8: Well, How Do I Look?

(Appearance And Illusion) ................................... 143

Chapter 9: Shoot Straight Will Ya!

(Learn How To Shoot Well) ................................ 156

Chapter 10: You Sit In A Tree? You Have Got

To Be Kidding Me. (Tree Stands

And Blinds) .............................................................. 181

Chapter 11: I Have Ants In My Pants.

(Hunting On Foot) ................................................. 198

Chapter 12: Oh GREAT! Now What?

(Deer Recovery) ..................................................... 212

Chapter 13: Gut Deer? (Removing The

Organs That Most Of Us

Don't Want To Eat) ............................................... 223

Chapter 14: Come And Get It!

(Caping, Aging, Cutting

And Storing Your Meat) ....................................... 239

Chapter 15: Your Footprint Is Beautiful.

(Forest And Game Management

Through Enhancement And

Harvesting) .............................................................. 266

Chapter 16: Please Do Not Hate Me

(Public Relations) ................................................. 280

# Contents

Chapter 17: One Last Story (One Must

                End With A Success Story) ..................................... 289

Appendix: A Basic Hunter's Day Pack ...................................... 299

# Get Out Of The Arm Chair!
## (The Wilderness Outside Your Door)

*T*he predawn was still and cold. Frosty air stung my fingers as I slid my Mossberg 500 slug-gun over my right shoulder and placed three rounds in my coat pocket. Slipping my gloves on, I grabbed my day pack and began the short walk into the snow to the forest. The fresh three inches of powder looked curiously blue under the stars and the waning December moon. Other than my nose, I was cozy warm in my layered long underwear, fleece and hunting jacket. My headlight, strapped to my blaze orange baseball cap, shown ahead making the undisturbed top layer of snow crystals reflect dazzling colors, as though a diamond thief spilled his loot in a fast getaway.

There wasn't a sound. Stepping a few paces into the woods I paused to give thanks and to savor the moment. Entering the wilderness I tasted the timeless freedom of separation from "the daily concerns" for a while. I began my stalk, straining to see and hear farther and more acutely than humanly possible. Although I did not sense the deer at that moment, I knew they were around. Previous

27

scouting and hunts had assured me of that. My stalk was not super careful this time. I was distracted a bit by the beauty of the moment. Forsaking a real effort to blend and move with the forest, I drank in the cold night air and clear night sky just happy to be on my way to the hunt at dawn.

I slowed down just 50 yards from my tree stand. (A tree stand, is a set up where a hunter can comfortably spend time in a tree just a bit above the terrain where he can survey the area and hunt.) Another step, slowly adding my weight onto that foot, pausing, listening, gazing. . . As I closed to within 30 yards of my stand my eyes caught movement. I became like the tree next to me, perfectly still, just a part of the forest. Too bad I was so casual moments ago. A buck stood up to see what was approaching. I saw him clearly now, his antlers pale against the dense forest background. He was absolutely stunning. A little snow on his muzzle and on his back, accented his regal and perfect coat, and healthy physique. I had disturbed this fellow's rest. He froze, his eyes fixed on my headlight. I extinguished the light, realizing once again how adequately the moon and stars could light the predawn hour.

Mr. Buck was unsure what to do next, as was I. It would be another twenty minutes before first light and legal hunting hours. We peered at each other in the moonlight, he with the advantage. His vision, hearing and sense of smell were far greater than my own. Both of us were standing as still as possible. I knew what I was looking at, but he was not so sure. He raised his nose and lips to try to identify me by my scent. I was as de-scented as could be with just a hint of acorn cover scent on my boots. Still, he didn't like what he saw and turned to trot away. He knew something wasn't right. I had not obscured my form as I had approached, not expecting to find a buck bedded under my tree. I smiled, pleased to know my tree stand was in a good location, and I was also pleased to have had a close encounter with one of the most elusive and beautiful large game animals in our suburban forests. What made this encounter even more special is that I was in my back yard.

Yes, my back yard is a little piece of wilderness. Yours may be too, even if you do not have actual forest as part of your property. If you live in a rural to suburban town, and don't have a large dog or very tall fence, I can assure you that your back yard sees its share of game animals. If it does not, you are within minutes of a spot that does. We humans have pushed our way into forested areas, and because we like the forest and want to be good stewards, we often leave wooded acres between homes or even just narrow corridors of trees. Animals of all sizes can adapt to even the smallest natural habitats left undeveloped by man. They are "survivors" as my dad used to say. If there is a way to survive, they will find it.

When my wife and I purchased the land and built our home in Eastern Massachusetts, we suspected that there was some wildlife on our property and in the surrounding wooded environs. But if we had been told that there was a deer herd of roughly 18 deer per square mile as well as coyotes, foxes, fisher cats, muskrats, raccoons, beaver, turkeys, ducks, geese, egrets, herons, eagles, hawks, turtles, and more, on our property and surrounding land, we would probably have been skeptical. But with some basic tracking skills and just plain observation we have realized just how wild our suburban neighborhood is.

Prior to the 19th century Industrial Revolution, the majority of the acreage that was not forested was farmland. People lived very close to the land, giving and taking form it in balance. Humans and the natural world shared a connected and intimate relationship. For those who desire that harder but less complicated lifestyle, there are still many ways to live out parts of it. Personally, I wanted to experience wildlife in an intimate way. I learned a bit about wild edible plants. But it was hunting that really made me come alive and engage the natural world. Like anything else in life, if you want to know about something, you have to experience it and get involved.

I'm sure you have heard of the phrase; the "arm chair athlete". The armchair athlete often critiques the football or baseball star, making authoritative remarks about the coaching staff or referees. How many of these folks have actually played professional sports? How many of them really know what it is like to be a quarterback like Tom Brady and stand in the pocket while roughly 1,500lbs. of muscle, bone and sinew is trying to deck you before you can complete the pass. Do you get a rush like I do while watching a downhill skier in the Olympics, carve through the slalom or hold a beautifully controlled jump that keeps them airborne for what appears to be an eternity? It is certainly exciting to watch folks play a sport or perform a piece of complicated music or achieve some great human feat. But being a spectator is not nearly as powerful as being a participant. Let me tell you from personal experience, there is no greater way to connect with the wilderness than to spend time in it, letting your body and senses connect with it, giving and taking from it, and existing as an integral part of it - just as we were originally created to be.

Nobody invests more time, energy, money and passion into the improvement of wild lands and the health of animal species than hunters and wildlife management personnel. Successfully managed forests and herds are the result of hunters and the organizations they support. Humans have learned a lot over the years from the results of abuse of natural resources. We have been reaping the fruit of those before us who probably didn't know any better. But today we know how to take care of a forest and bring it to maturity faster than it could reach it on its own. Similarly, we can strengthen a herd every season by the way we carefully choose to harvest animals, and improve their habitat. Hunting is like pruning a fruit tree to help it to bear more and healthier fruit. In both cases we are giving AND taking from nature. Today, organizations such as the Rocky Mountain Elk Federation, Ducks Unlimited, Pheasants Forever, National Wild Turkey Federation, Honored American Veterans Afield and small state run Departments of Fisheries and Wildlife monitor, guard and build up dozens of species. Hunting fees go directly to support and protect habitats and wildlife. So let me encourage you for your sake, for posterity's sake and for the good of our ecosystem; get dirty, get out of the arm chair and hunt in the local suburban woodlands as well as in the deep wilderness of our national forests. Pay your dues financially, physically and figuratively. Spend time acquiring knowledge, developing skills, and logging experience. The rewards are astounding. If you are reading this, I'd say you are on your way!

This book is dedicated to whitetail hunting. Although there are many other species to hunt and trap, we'll concentrate on one of the favorites. If you are like me you will branch out from there. But I always come back to whitetail hunting. It may be because the meat is so delicious and healthy. It may be that one kill yields so many wonderful meals. It may be the environment in which they live. I hope you will find some reasons for yourself. We'll explore this unique adventure in the chapters to follow.

We whitetail hunters have it good. Deep forests, far from human sprawl, will have great hunting areas. However, odds are the elusive whitetail is walking just outside your bedroom window at night and watching you do your yard work by day. After you establish that the deer are in your neighborhood you can start enjoying local hunting that will yield experiences that will thrill your heart, fill your freezer, adorn your den and give you great memories of not only the deer that you brought home but also the ones that got away! In the following pages you will learn to do all that and leave the forest healthier than when you entered it.

I would be remiss not to mention that suburban hunting requires extra care to do it safely and legally. Be sure to take a well-recommended hunter safety class and research all the local game laws as well as bylaws in the towns you wish to hunt. Your local game warden, environmental police and department of fish and game are ready to help.

# 2

# Deer Don't Fly!
## (Deer Sign)

*W*e were just finishing dinner and cleaning up. The sun had been down for about an hour. The phone rang. It was my cousin Steve. "Joe, I swear I got a clean shot just before dark, but I can't even find a track in the snow where I shot the deer! I swear I didn't imagine the whole thing. I shot a buck at dusk but when I got out of the tree, there was not even a mark on the snow where he was standing or anywhere! I'm not crazy. Can you help me track it?" I knew he wasn't imagining the event. He may be my "crazy" cousin but I knew that deer tracking can be tricky, especially after dark. And with the coyote packs in the forest where this deer was shot, it would not be wise to wait until morning. Coyotes in that area had a way of leaving little more than bones for the hunter who waited too long to recover his deer.

I put on some warm clothes and grabbed a lantern, marking tape and my compass. At the trail head stood my cousin, a big broad-chested, bearded outdoorsman with experience and determination. His home is adorned with pelts and mounts from his years of success hunting whitetail deer, bear and coyote. Steve is also an accomplished fisherman. But right now his eyes were showing a combination of frustration with the lack of evidence of a kill and relief that I was willing to help him find his downed animal. "Thanks for coming. I know I shot one. There is no way I missed. I sited the gun in this week and this shot was only about 25 yards," he barked, trying to convince himself that he was not going crazy. "There is not even a mark in the snow. How is this happening?!" We walked in the woods a short way as I pumped the white gas lantern to life and gently interjected, "Let's take a look cuz'. I'm just happy to get out tonight." Turning back to the trailhead, he mumbled, "There have to be tracks. Last time I checked, deer don't fly."

We hiked quietly, Steve leading the way. The sky was clear and there was no moon. The stars were bright above the leafless, snowy branched canopy. We arrived at his stand and he climbed in. We planned to have him get back into the stand and "talk me" to the place where he shot the deer. That way, I would be standing where the deer was and the prints would be clear. I cranked the gas on the lantern up to full. The cold was starting to chill my gloved fingers and my exposed nose. There were about two inches of fresh snow on the ground from the day before so I was confident that this was going to be a piece of cake. But what we found was surprising and challenging.

Steve directed me away from his stand to a distance of about 30 yards. This put me over the swamp which was frozen solid with a pristine, thin blanket of snow. The only obstructions were sap-lings poking through the ice. Each sapling was about 6 feet tall, with trunks and branches measuring from a half inch to one inch in diameter. These saplings were brushy at the top and poked through the ice with a density of roughly one sapling per square foot—quite tricky to navigate in the dark, even with a lantern. Steve patiently yelled out instructions to direct me to the spot where he remem-bered the deer had been standing when he took his shot. When I arrived where he wanted me, he hollered, "Well? What do you see?" I looked around at the snow, doing my best not to damage any existing prints with my boots, although at this point I had found none. I swung the lantern around between the saplings, astonished that I could not find a single impression in the snow. "Are you sure this is where the deer was?" I asked sheepishly. For the first time, I began to wonder if he indeed did imagine the deer encounter. "That is the spot. Come on, there has to be a track! Man, why can't we see anything?!" I took a couple of steps beyond where he put me along the line of his shot in the hope that he misjudged the distance in the dark. Nothing. The snow was untouched and the saplings even had snow all over their branches indicating that they were undisturbed. A little further, I spotted a tiny reflection in the snow, almost like a small piece of ice about the size of a corn kernel. I studied it just because there was no other mark on the snow to be found. It was perfectly white and shiny with a tiny red dot. Now that was odd. Taking my glove off, I reached down and picked it up. It stained my finger. BLOOD! This was a tiny piece of bone, likely a rib. I called to my cousin. "Cuz! I have blood. Come on down!" Steve dropped out of the tree and crashed his way to me. "Easy does it; we don't have a bearing really," I stated. I softened my delight, not wanting to get him too excited. Shining his flashlight on it, he took the fleck of bone from me.

Now we were both convinced that there was a wounded deer in the area. "Ok" I said, still unsure why there were no hoof prints in the snow. "In what direction did it run?" He pointed and intoned, "That way." Emphatically I insisted, "You stay here and I'll have a look. Don't lose this spot. It is our first clue to this deer's blood trail." My cousin respected my methodical and patient tracking abilities. And I, respecting his years of experience beyond mine as a hunter, knew better than to assume I could take charge of the track of his deer without his approval. "Go," he said.

I walked slowly in the direction he indicated. I scanned left and right, taking one step, looking, another step, and looking. Finally, after a full ten yards, I found a complete set of prints; all four hooves. These impressions in the snow were of a deer bounding away! The direction of the prints clearly indicated that the deer had been standing closer to the tree when shot than Steve had judged in the dark. Pointing my finger back to where the bounding tracks indicated the deer had come from, Steve moved and found where the deer had been standing for the shot. Great! Now we had a starting point and a look at the prints before the shot. We were on our way.

Steve walked to where I was standing, and I proceeded to look for the next set of prints. Moving along, I saw branches on the saplings where the snow may have been knocked off. But with the light of the lantern it was hard to be certain. I walked on, pushing through the saplings. A full 15 yards away, I found where the deer touched the ground again. Wow. He was leaping through and over the saplings. I called Steve to this next track. No blood was on the snow. Another 15 or so yards and slightly to the right was another set of hoof prints. This time there was a bit of blood spray to the left of the prints. This continued for about 60 yards where we found a spike buck, a buck with two small antlers, lying still on the ice. This deer had only touched the ground four times in that distance before dropping dead. That made the track challenging. He was a large deer. We high-fived and hooted a bit.

After celebrating, my cousin pulled out his license and removed the buck tag at the perforation. He filled out the date and signed it. Next, he stuffed it into the deer's ear and secured the ear closed with an elastic band. What a beautiful evening in the woods, and what a great outcome! Dragging the deer over the snow and ice was a pleasure. Steve did the most of it. We found a clear spot and he dressed it out.

Now that was not a typical track by any means, but it was a remarkable learning experience. I'll never forget the feeling of disbelief when we initially could not locate the track on the easiest medium there is—fresh snow. It proved once again to me that every hunt is different and so is every track. And, like a lot of things in life, what looks like an easy job might just turn out a bit more complicated than expected.

I have a friend and avid deer hunter named Chuck who used to say, "Deer are everywhere, just not all the time." Sounds obvious, right? But think about it for a moment. When we choose a location in which to hunt whitetails, we want our odds of encountering the deer to be high. So, before one hunts an area, he should be certain that the quarry is living in the area or at least passing through relatively often. Sometimes this is as easy as looking out the window. Other times one has to be a bit more of a detective and know what to look for. Deer, like most animals, leave very specific clues about their size, age and sex. These clue sets are called "deer sign" (a singular noun). Experienced trackers can gain insight into the animal by studying these clues. We will discuss that in detail further along in the chapter. But I want to encourage you. Start small and observe. Like everything else we practice in life, the more we do it, the better we become. Deer sign that you do not even recognize now, and you may have often passed by, will jump out at you one day, and can make the difference between filling your freezer with wild game or not. Tracking is a science and an art form. It takes time to learn how to do it and a lot of practice before it becomes second nature. I will offer you some things to look for that may motivate you to study bits of evidence that can be gathered from a whitetail deer track. I must add a caveat. These are general principles and will not always hold true because there are many things that can influence a track, such as different deer behaviors and personality or even an individual deer's physical characteristics such as a past injury or genetic variation. I have been tracking for many years but do not consider myself an expert by any means. I am observant, patient, and teachable. That has served me well. I have tracked with people who don't take the time to see anything. I've also tracked with people who have made me feel quite impaired in my abilities. Being a good tracker will help you as a hunter just as being a good putter will help you to become a good golfer. You may have heard the saying in golf, "Drive for show and putt for dough." The hunter's version of the saying is: "Shoot for show and track for dough." Tracking is that important. Your success in hunting will be directly linked to your ability to read the forest. There is no magic pill. Study and practice!

A survival instructor has crafted an inexpensive method for determining what animals inhabit your prospective hunting area or even your back yard: a "track patch". The track patch is a man-made section of loose soil that accepts animal footprints easily. It is a great tool for the beginner tracker that can be put together effortlessly in less than an hour. Hunters of all levels enjoy discovering and interpreting the valuable information collected on the patch. Start by finding a portion of level ground in the area of interest.

Before we start digging up our track patch, let us think strategically for a moment. Animals will notice even small changes to their environment. Stark changes and unusual appearances of food will cause them to be wary. Picture this. It is normal to see a blueberry pie on the kitchen counter, but not on the floor next to the bathroom door. We would happily help ourselves to the pie where we might expect to find it but not in the latter location. Similarly, we need to think of the outdoors as the animal's home. Subtle and natural changes on the edge of the woods will keep animals more relaxed than major excavations in the center of a trail. The plot should be just a little off the beaten path and away from wide open areas. Animals know a "set up" when they see it. Establishing a track patch in a transition area between forest and field, thicket and lawn is best.

Break up the soil of a roughly six by six foot square patch of earth. Next, till it with a tiller or by hand with a shovel. Do this until the soil has the appearance of chocolate cake mix. Then smooth it down just a bit with a tamp or a piece of plywood. Gather up some treats for your critters such as, cracked corn, bird seed (sunflower is excellent), an apple, some lettuce and even a big dollop of peanut butter. Now, wash your hands thoroughly and rub them with some pine needles or grass to give them a non-human scent. Most wild animals fear and avoid human beings. So the success of your experiment depends on not leaving your scent in the track patch, on the food, or in the surrounding area. This awareness of scent control will carry over into the hunt as well. We will discuss scent control in detail in a later chapter.

Place the peanut butter and other goodies in a circle at the center of the patch. Keep everything close to the center of the patch so that the critters need to step on your loosely packed dirt leaving beautiful, telltale paw, hoof or foot prints. Check on the patch the next day. Be patient. It may take several days, but you will find impression in the soil!

Preparing the "Track Patch"

So, what can we learn from this little patch of dirt? First, with the help of field guides, we can identify each animal that steps into our plot. We can also learn what they like to eat. By leaving the prints undisturbed and observing them over time we become familiar with the differences between fresh and old prints. We see how they age and are affected by weather and temperature cycles. This is very important for determining how often animals come through and how near they might be. It also sharpens our track-reading skills for prints we will come across in the wilderness.

There is a good educational exercise that I would like to share with you regarding how to learn to determine the age of a track. This method involves sustained daily observation and detailed recording of changes. In the off season, when scent is less of an issue, go to your track patch. Take a two-by-two inch block of wood and press it into the track patch. Record the date and the weather conditions in a notebook and observe the block's imprint. Take a photo of the block's "track" and paste the image into the notebook. Come back daily to observe, record and photograph what happens to the impression. When you arrive each day, create another impression with your wooden block a couple inches to the right of your first block imprint. Each day, take note of all new impressions appearing in the track patch, both from the animals and your manmade imprints. Keep going until you make impressions all the way around your track patch. Just look at how much those tracks change! As you study them, your mind will be training itself for accurate interpretations of other natural tracks that you see in the future. With practice you will be able to determine the age of most tracks.

When you have a little money to spend, and you feel the desire for a high tech gadget, consider buying a trail camera. This is a weatherproof camera that is strapped to a tree or fencepost. It has a thermal sensor to detect when a warm-blooded animal has come into its field of view. Day or night, depending on the settings, the camera will photograph what passes in front of it. A trail camera with an infrared flash does not spook the animals as much as the standard flash. Keep that in mind when making your purchase because a less expensive flash trail camera can drive wild game away. The camera is a fun toy and quite useful. Because today's models are digital you can take the photo card and observe your wild friends on your personal computer. The date and time is recorded on the photos so you can gather some interesting information. Later in this book you will learn how to remove your scent from the camera. I have photos of deer snouts giving the camera a good long sniff.

Whitetails leave many different signs, which makes these one of the easiest animals to track. First, we can find their cloved hoof print on almost any surface. The hard, narrow hoof and the deer's weight will make an indentation in nearly every medium. Certainly you can see the print in dirt but with a lot of study and practice, you will see their prints on your driveway where dust or pollen is the tracking medium. Behind the cloved portion of the hoof are two dew claws. Heavier deer and deer walking on very soft mediums may leave a track that will show the pair of dew claws behind the heart-shaped hoof.

We will discuss a variety of deer prints below. Each one tells us some characteristics about the animal. Most of the time, we don't have the pleasure of tracking on beautifully smoothed and prepared dirt or snow, but whenever this ideal surface occurs it is a great place to establish the basic skills. Take advantage of learning what you can from every print you see. I want to repeat that! Study every impression you see in detail. Your conscious and sub-conscious mind will pick up information that it will store. This information may get you a deer years from now that you would not have been able to track as a beginner.

Once you can see the more obvious tracks, start looking at the more difficult mediums such as the lawn. When tracking through a field of tall grass, the pushed down pathways can stand out quite a bit. Tracking is different on shorter grass. You do not just stare straight down at the lawn. Try this technique. Put the sun directly in front of you or directly behind you. Then focus your eyes at a sharp angle to the lawn. The tracks will appear either lighter in color or darker in color than the rest of the lawn. You will be amazed at how the lawn holds human and animal tracks for quite some time, until rain or temperature cycles relax the grass. The forest floor, typically covered with leaves, will give you another practical tracking experience. In this case, look for where the pressure was released from the leaf bed after the hoof moved away. Observe turned up leaves caused by hoof drag or lift. With forest litter, you must look for disturbed leaves, broken twigs and material moved about. In all cases, when time permits, do not move forward along the track until you find EACH print. This is an important exercise. Do not rush along. Each one of the places where the track changes the surface of the ground gives information about the animal. Some places where the foot leaves its mark will be harder to see, but by following the pattern of the past foot falls you will have a very good idea of where the next foot fall should be. If individual prints hold a host of information then viewing the patterns of multiple prints of the same animal will tell you even more.

Medium to small deer track

One characteristic of the whitetail's print is that its size is closely related to the size of the animal—the larger the deer, the larger its hooves. The best way to learn this is by observing the animal and then later, observing the tracks it has left behind. Another thing to look for is the spread of the split hoof. Very small deer will show very little spread in the hoof when walking. Do note that when the animal runs or leaps the hooves will splay a bit more. Often a fawn or yearling (a young deer under one year old) will stay close to the mother doe for a large portion of its first full year of life. Remember that deer are born in the spring. Although independent by late summer, yearlings will take comfort in the social circle that usually includes the mother. Thus it will be common to find the larger set of tracks from the mother along with the smaller set of tracks made by the younger deer. Observe this. It is rare to see mature bucks spending much time with yearlings. Note that the mother's track will be a bit larger and also show a more pronounced split in the hoof. If you find a large set of prints with a smaller set of prints staying close by, odds are the larger deer is a doe.

Rear hoof placed almost directly into front hoof print

Splayed hoof print of a bounding deer that I startled

When a mature deer walks, it will place its rear hoof, almost directly into the front hoof's print but not perfectly. The only animals I know of that place their rear foot directly into their front foot's print while walking are cats and foxes. Again there can be exceptions to this print overlap caused by the health of the animal and other variables. This partial overlay of the rear hoof over the front hoof print is observed only when the animal is walking, as opposed to trotting, cantering, loping, bounding or galloping. A walking mature doe will have her rear hoof fall a bit behind and outside the front hoof's track. The probable cause for this is the slightly flared pelvis of the doe's anatomy for birthing.

With a buck the opposite is observed. He will place his rear hoof just behind the front hoof print. However, some trackers have stated that a mature buck's broad chest and narrow pelvis result in the rear hoof landing to the inside of the front hoof print. Although I have seen these track patterns, I have also seen the same deer leave rear hoof prints that fall to the inside and outside of the front print! So while I can use relative front and rear hoof placement to help me determine the sex of an animal, it is only one piece of evidence. To be sure, it is wise to keep your eyes open for more.

Make a point of observing the walls formed by the hoof print. They contain information just as the floor of the impression does. Upper body movements, such as the turning of the head or shifting of the weight, can be deduced from the wall of the track. Even while just standing still, the movement of the upper body, head and neck will result in a small shift of the hoof below, impacting the walls of the track. A head turn to the left will result in a slight twist in the left front hoof. Nervous movements such as lowering the body in preparation for running away will appear in the track as well. The track walls will spread farther apart as the hoof shudders under the balancing animal. This is subtle stuff and won't be easily determined on most mediums. But look for it! The more you observe and study the more information you will glean from the track.

In addition to tracks, deer leave behind other clear signs of their presence. One of the least pleasant but certainly informative signs is their waste. Generally, deer tend to stand still while urinating. If you can detect either by scent or careful observation of the forest floor that a deer has urinated in an area, check the orientation of the tracks with respect to the urine spot. In snow this is easy, but print orientation is also discernible on dry forest floor. You may notice three things about hoof prints formed during urination: the rear hooves become side by side, are spaced wider apart, and point away from each other slightly. Some deer will curve their back when urinating. Others will do nothing different. Bucks will tend to have the urine spot notably ahead of the rear hooves while the does will urinate directly between or just behind the rear hooves.

Mounds of deer droppings are not only more obvious then urine, they are also teeming with helpful information. These do not tell you the sex of an animal, as far as I know, but they do tell you quite a bit about the size of the animal and its comfort level. First, let us consider the autumn droppings. The round droppings or Tic-Tac size and shape droppings are from a yearling. Oval droppings that are one centimeter long are from a more mature deer. Stool pellets that are just under two centimeters are from a big deer. As a beginner, when you find fresh droppings, return to the area often to learn how they age. Break a pellet each day to note how moist it is. Deer droppings will be moist or dry on the outside depending on the weather conditions. But the inside will generally be moist when they are fresh. As they age they become dry and crumbly. If you break apart a pellet and see that it is dusty on the inside, then you have found a very old one. Soon you will be able to determine the age of droppings by this repeated visitation and break up of one of the pellets in the pile. Of course, this is very useful when trying to determine if an area is being used right now or if the droppings are a month or even a year old. Generally a moist and shiny exterior indicates that the droppings are very fresh. However droppings that are moist from dew or rain do not shine. Droppings that are dry but easily squished are a few days to a week old. Droppings that are brittle are older still. Droppings that have lost their smoothness and distinct Tic-Tac shape are as much as a year old. Personal observation of a set of droppings over time could make you an expert on aging in just one season. Consider taking fresh droppings home in a baggie, and place them in your backyard where you can more conveniently observe their aging process.

Spring droppings sometimes clump

Fresh droppings from a small deer

Droppings found in spring and summer will tend to clump together almost to the point that you will not see the oval shaped pieces. As spring draws to a close, the droppings will become separated. This change in pellet appearance is caused by the variation of the deer's diet throughout the year. Deer are very adaptable and will eat everything from grass, leaves, moss, fungus and berries in the summer to nuts, leaves, twigs and late season fruit in the autumn. During the winter deer dig for food under the snow as well as eating the buds and twigs on saplings. They will also consume bark, cedar leaves and other surprising "leftovers" from the growing season. The spring will provide the succulent, tender greens again and the cycle will continue. Each season's "Bambi buffet" generates evidence of deer presence. Look at the tips of low tree branches and short greenery. Are the tips nibbled off? Are there little holes in the ground where plants have been uprooted?

Deer droppings indicate, to some extent, how relaxed a deer is. Deer do not tend to relieve themselves when they are uneasy or nervous. Maybe you can relate to this. I know I sure can. If you find a pile of droppings, it is likely that the deer is happy and comfortable in the area. If you find lots of dropping piles in one area, you have promising evidence for two possibilities: an individual deer spends a lot of time there, or multiple deer are gathering there. Further study of other deer sign such as tracks and beds will help you determine how many deer have made this their "hang out". This brings up another significant deer sign—one that is probably the most indicative of a comfortable animal—the deer bed. Deer lie down, or bed down, for many reasons. Like us, they need to rest and conserve energy whenever possible. Always keep an eye out for a kidney-shaped impression on the ground, grass, leaves or snow. This is a "bed." Put the back of your hand on the surface to see if it is warm. You may have just frightened off the deer as you approached. Although deer do not rest in the same place daily, they do tend to return to certain bedding areas. There are a variety of reasons why deer prefer a certain spot: it keeps them hidden from view or protected from wind, or it is close to food. All this information will be useful for you. Keep tracking.

Ah but the really exciting signs that I like to see are the ones generated exclusively by bucks in the late summer and autumn!

These are rubs and scrapes left by "rutting" bucks! What is a rutting buck? The "rut" is an interesting term related to the deer mating season. Before we can understand the rut, we need to know a bit more about bucks. Despite their size and strength, bucks are rather timid and careful animals. Have you ever heard the saying "Fools rush in where angels fear to tread."? Well, the bucks are the "angels" in this analogy. They don't go anywhere without first conducting a thorough scan with all the senses. They hide and move very stealthily. Often bucks will be in an area and even under your nose but you will see only the does. To see the bucks, you must be more patient, more observant, and more stealthy than they are. However, they get a bit bolder and maybe even a bit careless when they have breeding on their mind. As the rutting season approaches, the does, though not yet ready to mate, begin to release pheromones—biological chemicals attractive to the opposite sex. The bucks, in turn, begin to seek out the receptive does. I like to call this time "pre-rut" because of the bucks' ritualized "courting" of females long before actual mating occurs. Thus, by definition, the rutting season consists of the courting and mating stages. Depending on your location, the time that the rut begins and ends will vary. Generally the rut begins two to four weeks after the autumnal equinox.

There are some known and unknown factors that come into play in determining when the rut begins. Numerous hunters have posited theories on how to predict it. Some use the moon phase relative to the autumnal equinox, while others factor in the temperature. Some theories consider barometric pressure combined with the length of the day light hours. Frankly I don't claim to know who is right or wrong. I can't even make sense of all the theories and research. And after reading the hunting magazines, listening to old timers, and spending over a thousand hours in the woods scouting and hunting, I have decided that predicting the rut really isn't as critical as being able to detect it! So here are my general guidelines and indicators that I believe will help you determine when "pre-rut" has started and when the full blown "rut" is on, as well as "the second rut" (which will be explained at the end of this chapter.)

A fresh rub                    Last year's rub

Now let's go back into the woods and make some more observations. Let's look for "rubs" — bare spots on tree trunks resulting from a buck that has rubbed his antlers against them and stripped off the bark. These are noticeable on all types of trees from saplings the size of broom stick handles to mature trunks as thick as your forearm. There are instances when deer will rub far bigger trees, but that is less common. Rubs can be observed anywhere from knee height to belt height or higher depending on the size of the deer. This is both a "pre-rut" and "rut" activity. Why is he doing this? Once again there are theories of all kinds. Some say it is because the buck wants to rub off the antlers' outer velvet. But I have seen a buck with bare bone white antlers work a sapling with a vengeance. There was no velvet left on him. Some say he is building neck muscles. When he challenges other bucks, he'll need strong neck muscles to prove his right to territory and does. Perhaps strong neck muscles make him look "buff" to the ladies. Many believe that bucks leave scent on the trees as a form of communication to other bucks in the area and to the does as well. It may be like a calling card: "This is my travel corridor; this is my little cluster of trees. Willing does please come; other bucks stay out." However, as I mentioned before, it is more important to me to gather information that I can use, than to burn up all my mental energy trying to determine the reasons that bucks do this. Therefore, take note of the following: Are the rubs that you find fresh? Do they exude an odor and appear to have been done recently? Are there many of them in an area? Or are they forming a line through the forest? These observations help you decide how you hunt this area, if you decide to hunt it at all. If there is a cluster of rubs, you may want to get down wind and find some shooting lanes to the area of the rubs. If there is a line of rubs through the forest, you have an excellent idea of the travel route of this buck.

In my experience, one cannot determine the size of the buck by the size of the tree that is rubbed. My trail camera and my direct observation have revealed that bucks of all sizes rub trees of all sizes. What identifies the size of the deer is how much of the tree is rubbed. Vertical rubbings over a foot long indicate big deer. The longer the antlers and neck, the longer the rub on the tree will be. A somewhat less reliable determiner of buck size is the height at which the rub is located on the tree. A mature deer stands taller than a young deer, and his rub will naturally be higher. With time, observation and thoughtful interpretation you will gain valuable information from trees that will help you in your hunt, even if you don't know exactly why the deer are rubbing.

An active scrape with
the typical broken branch above

Another sign to be looking for is the "scrape". Though primarily a rutting indicator, it can also be found during the pre-rut phase. A scrape is a portion of ground that has had the top layer of debris scraped away to expose the earth below. Bucks will drag their hooves over the ground and stomp leaving scent from their tarsal glands as well as their urine. Scrapes that are only a couple of feet long tend to be a sign of a large buck. Ironically, the smaller bucks go crazy in scrapes and will clear areas that sometimes exceed the length of their bodies. Bucks often scrape where there is an overhanging branch. They will slash the branch above with their antlers, maybe leaving scent there as well. A scrape is another form of communication similar to the rub, but it is all about scent.

Although these scrapes are initiated and maintained by bucks, the does will visit these spots and leave their scents too. The bucks communicate with each other in these scrapes; the larger bucks leave more scent and therefore establish their dominance. The bucks will also pick up on the does' scents and time their visits to encounter the females who frequent the site. I've been trying for years to hunt over scrapes and have even created mock scrapes with scent lures. My trail camera has showed me that most of the visits to the scrape by deer of either sex are at night. However some visits are in the day and those are the ones we need to capitalize on. When a scrape is visited often, we say that it is an "active scrape". You will be able to determine how active it is by using your nose and eyes. In autumn as the leaves are slowly drifting down from the trees, it is easy to identify how long ago the scrape was made or maintained by observing how many new leaves have fallen over it. Later in the season when the trees are bare, I will place leaves over the scrape and check the following day to see if they have been cleared away. By then there is usually no activity. In either case, observe the cleared area and look for prints. As stated before, impressions made in the scrape indicate who has been visiting and how long ago they were there. Last, but not least, take a good sniff. Without leaving your scent in the scrape or surrounding area, get your nose down in there and try to pick up a scent. Buck urine and doe-in-heat urine smell very different. Since odors cannot be easily described in print, I suggest that you purchase various whitetail scent lures and become familiar with them. They are an important part of a deer hunter's arsenal. I'll let you know how to use those scents later.

By using the autumnal equinox plus two to four weeks as a general rule, you can estimate the transition date between pre-rut and rut. Remember that there are variations in every system, especially one as complex as our environment. Furthermore, deer are not hormonally programmed to go into heat simultaneously at 12:00am Monday morning. And all the bucks are not going to get "the itch" to rut at the same moment either. Expect variations in the dates and the individual deer. But do look for the rut evidence.

The rut is a special time for the hunter as well as the deer. While the bucks are rubbing the saplings in the pre-rut, there will be lots of does running away from these courting males. However, when the rut is in full swing, the does may actually be harder to find for a time. Does will "stand," meaning they will stay put in the thick areas. This signals their receptiveness to the bucks that will be all too eager to tend to them. Rut-crazed bucks feverishly seeking receptive females will respond to manmade decoys, scent lures and audible calls. (We will talk more about those types of tactics in later chapters.) When the deer are distracted by the rut, we hunters gain an advantage.

This brings us to the late season. In the event that some of the does do not become pregnant during the rut, there is a post-rut period ("second rut") where those females will be in estrus again. This will occur about three weeks after the peak of the rut. The bucks that still have energy from all the running, chasing and tending of does will be on the move a little longer to find those remaining receptive ones. While hunters can enjoy success during this second rut, they will observe less activity and fewer deer for the taking. If you see does darting about or looking over their shoulders, keep under cover, and be on the lookout for Mr. Buck in case you still have a buck tag to fill out. If the law says you can take the doe, this is probably one of your last chances to do so. The hunting season is ending soon, and all deer will have their stomachs in mind. They will be eating as much as possible unless the snows are deep; then the deer will be conserving energy instead. For whitetails, conserving energy looks a whole lot like laziness. When they are not eating, they will be resting in thickets or bedded down on south-facing hills to take up the sun's heat. In general they won't want to run or even travel much except to avoid predators and find more food. Keep that in mind when planning a late season hunt.

In addition to the whitetail signs described here, there are countless other types of sign left by deer throughout the year. It would take many chapters to describe them all and their variations in presentation. But let me suggest that you might notice nibbled ends of branches where the deer have eaten the buds. You may find hair pulled off as a deer walks beneath a low branch. If you are observant you will notice more each time you look for deer sign. Some days you will discover that deer have visited some surprising places. I've found signs on a little island in the middle of a big lake or on the yew beside the front door at the general store. The signs are everywhere, and with practice you will become skilled at spotting and interpreting them.

# 3

# WOW! What A Big Brain
## (Deer And Human Abilities)

*C*rack! It was the sound of a large stick breaking in two under the hoof of a very large deer. I knew that sound, and this time it actually startled me. Ok, so I had been sitting quietly in the tree for over an hour and was so comfortable I must have dozed off a bit. It is rare, but it happens. My eyes opened and my heart rate began to climb. I strained to put all my senses on full alert while thinking to myself, "Relax Joe, do your inventory, then locate the deer." I glanced down to my bow, my left hand on the handle, and an arrow nocked on the string. Glancing left with my eyes only, I began slowly standing up from my sitting position. Typically I locate the source of the sound first to be sure I'm not being watched but having been caught snoozing, I figured it was time to cut a corner. I saw some motion about 70 yards away. A very large-bodied buck was coming toward my tree. He paused, clearly oblivious to my presence. Using his thick, white, eight point set of antlers, he casually lifted a downed branch that was across the path. Imagine that, a deer that liked to keep his run clear of debris. This buck was one of the largest deer I had ever seen and would be the largest deer I ever harvested, should things work out. Taking advantage of his casual demeanor, I readied myself, adjusting my feet into a comfortable shooting stance. I set my release aid and hooked it to the string. Mr. Buck turned and began to move behind me. He slowed his movements and grunted. He was attracted to the doe-in-heat scent that I had hanging on a sapling branch just 10 yards from my tree.

Big deer don't get big by being foolish. This fellow was no exception. He began to suspect that something was not right. He believed a doe was close by, but she did not respond to his grunt. His eyes scanned the area, yet could not see the young lady whose musky scent wafted in his sensitive nose. I believe he detected a "set up". Turning to his right, he came around behind my tree stand. He stopped in very close proximity with his left side facing the trunk and my back.

After about 20 minutes of silence and no movement on his part, I slowly peeked over my shoulder to see him facing me perfectly. He stared right into my eyes and didn't move a muscle. He was on to me. Directly behind my tree, he was in an impossible location to be shot with the bow even if he turned to expose his heart. This wasn't working out well at all. I froze all movements except my heartbeat. I even started to be careful with my breathing not wanting the vapor from by breath to be visible. "What's the use?" I wondered. "Clearly he saw me!" Because my neck was getting stiff from holding this awkward position, I slowly twisted my head back so I was looking straight ahead. I strained to hear his movements and hoped he would come around the tree to investigate the odd creature up there. Listening intently for him to move, I waited for about 30 minutes. I was in disbelief that this buck would not move for such a long time. Not able to take it any longer, I once again, with the slowness of clock hands, peeked back through the tree at him. To my amazement he was gone. He had arrived looking cool and casual in his quest for a mate. However at the first sign of trouble, he slipped away quietly like thistle down caught in a gentle breeze. I scanned my entire perimeter slowly and carefully, seeking and listening. Surely he had to be nearby. But no. Mr. Old, Fat and Handsome would live on. Clearly he was exceptionally aware and wise. He didn't get that mature, large and fully-antlered by allowing himself to be hunted.

If you ever shoot a large buck with a wonderful set of antlers, you will likely want a photo of yourself holding up the rack! You may even have the head mounted on your wall in the den. Why do we do that? Because the antlers are one of the impressive and endearing attributes of the deer. Obviously, it is not possible to mount the deer's keen sense of smell or super hearing on the wall for posterity. Coyotes and foxes have their soft, beautiful pelts from which we can make gloves, hats and wall hangings. But one cannot display a coyote's cunning or fox's stealth or their super senses. The photo of you with your buck won't show your skill set either. What I am getting at? That, as lovely and remarkable as these wild creatures are, YOU have gifts also. Having a less keen sense of smell or hearing does not put you at a great disadvantage on the animals' turf. Human gifts are better. You have been given a very powerful mind along with dexterity in your hands that your quarry cannot match. You have tools at your disposal—products of the human mind and hands—from your compass to your rifle, from your varied high tech clothing to your binoculars. You even have a freezer at home in which to store all the meat that you will harvest. You can think through, analyze, review history, learn from others, read stored knowledge from books, and make educated guesses about the future. Now that is impressive! Capitalize on the amazing mind that you have. Appreciate that your eyesight, hearing, and sense of smell, though dull compared to most animals, are still excellent. You will see. After I help you hone them, you will see better, hear better and even discern odors better. In truth, you are a gifted predator.

Deer have good eye sight. But of all their senses, this one is the least comprehensive. Deer can easily see a motionless person or animal positioned in an open area, but they cannot readily discern a stationary creature in busy surroundings such as foliage, even if the creature is only partially obscured. This limitation is balanced by unique visual strengths. Deer have an uncanny ability to detect a pair of eyes staring at them. They see well in the dark and notice the subtlest motion. However, this motion detection is not solely a result of the eye's performance. It is primarily a function of neurological processes that are instinctual and habitual to the deer. These capabilities allow the deer to be nocturnal when necessary and to perceive predators during the day or night.

What physical features of the eye account for the aforementioned uniqueness? The pupil of the deer's large eyeball is far bigger than the human pupil and therefore gathers significantly more light. The mirror-like retina in the rear reflects some of this light back out giving the light energy a second pass over the nerves. This makes the eyes seem to glow when we shine a light at them after dark. Deer eyes have a very high concentration of nerve structures called "rods" in their retina. Rods are very sensitive to light and dark but not color. They are especially useful in low light. We humans have far fewer rods in our retina, and therefore we have relatively poor night vision. One more factor makes the deer's eye very effective. The deer's range of vision has been found to reach partly into the ultraviolet portion of the light spectrum, beyond the human chromatic scale. Some people theorize that this somehow improves the deer vision at dawn and dusk. Deer also have structures known as "cones" in their retina which provide the deer with a weak perception of color. Studies have shown that orange and red hues are not detected well and appear as grey to the animal. However, this shortcoming is offset by the wide field of view made possible by the location of the eyes on each side of the head.

Let us consider human vision for a moment. Although human eyes are not super performers in the dark, our night vision can actually be improved with practice. Even though night vision is not critical for hunting because we do not hunt deer at night, it is worth mentioning that if we regularly allow our eyes to adjust to the dark, we can see reasonably well without artificial light. In other ways we have the deer beat with our vision. We have sensational predatory sight thanks to corrective lenses, a revolutionary product of the human mind. Furthermore, our eyes work together with the brain to determine distance with very high precision. This is crucial when addressing a target (deer) at various ranges. And when necessary, we can use binoculars to see details well beyond the scope of the naked eye. Our ability to discern the full spectrum of colors allows us to see a "camouflaged" animal despite the surroundings. I've lost count of the number of times I have watched a deer in her brown coat, standing still and "hiding" among the yellow autumn leaves of a beech tree. Have you ever watched a cotton tail rabbit sit perfectly still in a patch of clover or among the flowers? Again, the contrast of colors makes the animal stand out. If you were to see these things in black and white, as many animals do, the deer or cotton tail would indeed be far more hidden.

Now let's talk about motion. Here is the trick! As I said before, sensing motion is a neurological process. Simply put, detecting motion has far more to do with your mind than your eyes. It is imperative to be able to detect the smallest movements within the field of view to be a good hunter. Although it may sound odd, it is possible to sharpen your neurological "motion sensor" by practicing specific techniques. I am living proof that this is absolutely true. After briefly practicing the techniques described later in this chapter, I had trained myself to use my eyes to their maximum capabilities. You are wired to do this naturally so it is not going to be difficult to learn.

Our ability to see motion is directly related to how much of our field of vision we are using. Our eyes each focus multiple times per second in response to feedback from the brain. Our brains receive the "full field" of vision continually from both eyes. But modern life bombards us with endless optical signals, the majority of which we have trained ourselves to ignore since childhood. We tell ourselves, "Don't let this distract me." Consequently we are attentive only to a portion of what we see because our brains filter out most of the visual clutter. This learned response to sensory overload is commonly known as "tunnel vision." When we were young, the world was new and fascinating. To look at everything with unhurried curiosity was part of our natural learning process. This of course drove our time-conscious parents and teachers nuts. Eventually they required us to develop tunnel vision to avoid being distracted by the bird outside the window so we could concentrate in school. We learned how to do everything from reading books to operating a computer, without letting all the other signals around our peripheral vision grab our attention. But even though our brains do the filtering, our eyes first take in the original full field of view. While tunnel vision is a necessary life skill, there is a time to shut it off and switch to full field vision. When the brain begins to interpret this unfiltered view, several important changes will occur. First, you will obviously see more! And when hunting or just visiting the forest, this is a good thing. Second, you will experience a heightened sensitivity to motion within your view. Third, you will become more relaxed, because your eyes and brain were naturally set up to work most efficiently with full field vision. Lastly, this unfiltered view makes greater use of your subconscious mind. Uh oh. . . a bit more neurological science ahead. . . but you can handle it.

The subconscious mind is very good at absorbing information without special effort. We must work hard to get our conscious mind to memorize things, but our subconscious memorizes them automatically. A good example of the subconscious mind working behind the conscious occurs when I walk through an unfamiliar forest or city. If I must return to my starting point, it is sometimes difficult for me to remember the route and all the landmarks I passed. But as I walk back, my subconscious recalls all the sights I encountered and guides me right back to my starting point. My mind has recorded things I saw even though I did not make a conscious effort to memorize them. Like an organic digital camera, the subconscious mind "photographs" and stores a massive database of images for future retrieval. Using your full field vision will engage more of your mind's natural talents, a crucial aspect of becoming a better hunter.

How do you switch to full field vision? You probably realize it involves recapturing your childhood sense of wonder prior to tunnel vision. I'll just give you an exercise to get you back into it. With practice you will be able to switch back and forth as needed. It is more practical and fun to do this exercise outside rather than indoors because you need to have numerous things in your field of view. In other words, don't fill your vision with just a white wall or an empty ocean out to the horizon to do this exercise. Find a good vista with trees, grass and other things positioned close by and far away in the field of view.

Ready? Are you standing in a park? Are you standing before a piece of forest or in your very own back yard? Great! Now pick an object in the middle of your view, like a small pine tree, and stare at it. You are using tunnel vision at this point. Next, don't change your eyes at all. Relax and observe the bush on the left side of your field of view without moving your eyes; keep them pointed at the center of your vista! Examine this bush. You can see it, can't you? You can see its leaves, the color of its flowers, and its location relative to the center of the vista. Relax, blink, and continue to gaze straight ahead at the small pine tree. This type of vision feels different, does it not? It should feel comfortable.

While keeping your eyes ahead, see the rock in the peripheral vision of your right eye. Yes, you are looking straight ahead but you just saw a chipmunk scurry across that rock! You would not have seen that with your tunnel vision. Finally observe the bush on your left and the rock on your right at the same time. Blink, relax, it works – doesn't it? You should be able to observe everything to the left, the right, and above and below you all at the same time. You will notice something fantastic in this mode of seeing. You will begin to detect the slightest movements. If a deer flicks its tail, you won't miss it. If a fox turns his ear, you won't miss it. As I stated before, your unconscious mind is recording it all for playback to your conscious mind.

Play with this. Sit out in the woods for a while and view the world with your full field vision. A bird will not be able to cock its head without you noticing. A slight twitch of a squirrel's tail will catch your eye while he's perched on a branch 50 yards away. Oh yes, you are seeing far more now. You will be astonished at how sensitive and capable your vision is.

Let's go back to tunnel vision for a moment. This limited way of seeing can play a role in hunting, especially when we enhance it with binoculars. Most guys today refer to the use of binoculars as "glassing." For many years, I hunted without binoculars. In my suburban and sometimes rural settings, I thought I really didn't need them. After all, in the majority of my hunting environments, the density of the trees, the brush and even the contours of the land made it impossible to see beyond 75 yards. With the exception of some farm land where I can see hundreds of yards, I typically hunt wood lots. So why would I bother carrying binoculars? Well, after reading several hunting magazines that encouraged the short range use of binoculars I decided to give it a try. Because we are speaking about short range use, I'm not suggesting you go out and buy a pair of monster binoculars that weigh ten pounds and can easily see the little rocks that collect at the bottom of the craters on the moon.

My dad gave me a pair of navy binoculars like that built during WWII. They are excellent: crystal clear, very high magnification, and weather sealed, even though they probably don't have all the modern spectral compensation. They are great for bird watching or detecting a small boat out on the horizon in the open sea. But if you wear them around your neck too long you will need physical therapy for misaligned vertebrae!

There are some quality compact binoculars that fold tightly to fit into your coat pocket. They open easily even with gloved hands, and are so lightweight that when they are worn around your neck you will forget they are there. Don't overspend on a pair of binoculars because they will be taken into tough environments where they will likely get scratched, dropped or otherwise abused. On the other hand, a cheap set will disappoint you right away when you test them at the store. So find a balance between price and quality, and choose a pair that will serve your needs in any weather. Below is a brief overview of lens specifications to assist in your selection.

Much of what I am about to say here about the optical nomenclature of binoculars also applies to scopes for your gun, so keep that in mind. My own binoculars are made by Bushnell. They are 10x25 with a field of view of 302 feet at 1000 yards. The 10x indicates that the image viewed will appear to be 10 times nearer than it would look to your naked eyes. I find that 10x is fine for the short range hunting application. The aperture of the object lens, the lens closest to the object being viewed, is 25mm. Binoculars with large object lenses gather more light and so are brighter. These are better suited to low light conditions, but there is a tradeoff. The large object lenses are bulkier and heavier to carry. So consider smaller object lenses for this application.

The field of view is a function of multiple characteristics of the optics. It refers to the diameter of the viewing circle at a given range. For example, through my binoculars, a circular field of view with a diameter of 300 feet will be visible when I am looking at a flat surface 1000 yards away. For our application, that translates to roughly a 15-foot diameter at 50 yards. Good enough.

There are a few situations for which I have personally found glassing useful. Deer love to spend time in the cover of brush and thickets. They will lie down and blend into almost any surrounding. The binoculars virtually bring us so close to a deer's hiding spot that we cannot help but see the animal. I have scanned thickets at a distance of 40 yards with my eyes and not seen the camouflaged doe staring right at me. But when I glassed the thicket, I could see her and just about count the whiskers on her nose. As I lowered the binoculars, I could just barely detect her shape. The doe was confident that I was unaware of her position. That is an important point! If deer believe they are hidden, they will tolerate close proximity to human beings. While hunting with a gun this might give me a great opportunity to shoot. During archery season when my shooting range is about 30 yards or less, this proximity fact may not guarantee an immediate kill shot. After all, sneaking up to within 30 yards of a wild deer is not easy. It can be done, but there are far easier ways to ambush a deer which will be discussed later in chapter 10. Knowing where they like to hide helps determine where YOU want to hide.

Another circumstance for glassing is in the late season when it is too cold to spend time staying still waiting for the deer to come to you. In that case, you may find yourself moving stealthily through the woods, a skill known as "still hunting." This can be done during the most inclement weather conditions and is a super way to get close to game. The moving keeps you warm, and wind and rain obscure your noises and motions. Still hunting will be addressed in detail in chapter 11. Stopping occasionally to glass the surroundings during still hunting can help you track, locate or follow the deer.

When I am bow hunting from a tree stand I am not comfortable shooting a deer over 30 yards away. In this situation you might think that binoculars would not be very useful to me. But as a short range archer I don't count glassing out. Glassing enhances my ability to penetrate visually into the brush, and also provides an earlier warning of approaching deer, giving me more time to set up my shot.

Much more can be said about the complex biology of human vision. But that discussion belongs among scientists. For the hunter, understanding the basics of the sense of sight is sufficient. By taking a moment to be observant and by using your "full field" of view, you will see many more animals including your quarry!

Let us briefly examine a deer's exceptionally sensitive hearing. Deer can detect sounds that are not only below the human sound threshold, but also outside of our spectrum of hearing. By that I mean that deer will hear low volume sounds that we will not detect, and they will hear frequencies that are beyond our aural range. Additionally they know and respond to patterns of subtle sounds in the woods that we typically ignore. When our jacket slides gently against a twig, it might make a noise that is very high pitched, faint and seemingly insignificant to us. We may not even notice it. But the deer just went on high alert and is scanning our direction with peaked ears, nose and eyes. One time, I was watching a couple of does who suddenly went on high alert and were listening and looking intently down a fire lane through the forest. They became nervous and were clearly ready to bolt away. I listened and looked but could detect nothing. Ultimately, the deer decided to stalk away cautiously. About 5 minutes later, I glassed two people walking up the fire lane at a distance of roughly a quarter of a mile. Those deer knew humans were coming long before I did.

Earlier in this chapter, I explained how to "level the playing field of vision" between deer and hunter. I would now like to offer a similar discussion about the sense of hearing. Our ears detect and send large volumes of information to the brain. And, as with our eyes, a large portion of this information is filtered out and not brought to the conscious mind. We want to be more aware of all the sounds that our ears pick up. I call this "unfiltered hearing," the neurological process of examining more of what is heard and not just throwing the information away. In the hunting environment, it is imperative that you use your hearing to find the deer. They are stealthy, but they very often give away their approach audibly. I most often hear deer before I see them. Yes, I have good hearing, but it is not super human. Since deer have diverse personalities, some will walk with more care than others. If they are trying to be sneaky, and are stalking through the woods, they will be very silent. We want to sharpen our hearing as much as possible. If you are not hearing-impaired, you can improve your hearing in minutes simply by making a concentrated effort to listen carefully. There is a continuous concert in the forest. Ask yourself, "What is that sound?" Every sound in the forest has a source and brings a message. In some cases I have known when a hunting friend has entered the woods to join me from as far as a quarter mile away just by hearing how the crows or blue jays have scolded. Now that may seem remarkable, but it is not magic. When you visit the woods, stop and listen for extended periods of time and do nothing else. You will hear a myriad of sounds. Identify them if you can. Continue. Listen for the softest sounds as well as the loudest ones. Listen to the distant noises as well as those nearby. Cup your hands behind your ears and pick up the subtlest sounds. In a very short time, you will be aware of things happening around you that you didn't pay any attention to in the past.

The above exercise is simply a matter of slowing down to enter into a state of greater awareness. Everyone can do it. With practice you will soon be hearing the red squirrel and the birds telling you where ground-dwelling animals are moving about. You will become aware of other people in the woods. While stopped and listening, I have discovered families of voles just beneath the leaves at my feet. I have heard a fisher cat scratching a tree apart to eat the squirrels inside. I have detected a herd of deer moving through the brush, and I cut them off as they exited. Keener powers of hearing and sight will combine to make you a more successful hunter.

Now before you think I have gone off the deep end, regarding the use of senses, let me just remind you that deer are not easy prey. We want to use every advantage available, including the sense of smell. Yes, for most of us, smell is the least emphasized sense, the least sensitive, and as a result, the least utilized. Yet it is quite valuable in the hunt. Believe it or not, on one of my better days, I did smell a deer approaching. I don't think that my nose has ever significantly added to my success rate. But I have smelled deer, especially during the rut. They stink! After a shot, I have smelled the blood trail of a wounded deer. While this may sound disgusting, it is important to use all the information available to you. Start by sniffing the scrapes you find in the ground. They won't smell great but they will train you to recognize deer scent when present. Smell the rubs on trees. These are wonderful because bruised and broken bark give off the sweet scent of the inner live portion of the tree, just below the bark. You are an intelligent predator and your success will depend on how much you use your abilities. You have a powerful brain! It is your greatest hunting asset. Trust that your senses are powerful as well. There is a great predator in the woods. It is you.

# Hiding In The Open
## (Introducing the Four Dimensions Of Camouflage And How To Beat The Amazing Deer Senses)

*I* was stalking ever so slowly toward my tree stand deep in a 2000 acre wildlife management area. The forest is just around the corner from my home. About 300 yards into this piece of forest was one of my tree stands. I was really in the right mindset this sunny and mild autumn afternoon. For some reason it was easy that day to move so much like the forest around me. I stepped forward, toe pointed down through the blueberry bushes, rolling my weight slowly around the edge of my foot before committing, feeling for sticks, being sure to make the minimal amount of sound. When the breeze picked up I increased my pace. When the forest went silent and still, so did I. I had my appearance, my movements, my sounds and my scent camouflaged. Even my intentions were hidden, buried below my mind's quiet and unscheduled goal of reaching "the tree" without disturbing the forest any more than necessary. Time flowed for me that afternoon like it does for the animals. I existed in time, yes, but without measure. My only activities were simply living and hunting. That combination beats any modern stress management system. Eventually, I caught site of the tree I would climb. Slowly scanning and slinking, I made my way to it, unconcerned about the passage of time. I was pleased that I could hardly detect my own presence on my way through the forest. I was on my game. So much so that this hunt remains in my mind these many years later. I was hidden in the open.

It was late October. The weather was comfortable, just cool enough to keep the flying bugs away. The leaves had only partially fallen, and the beech trees were draped with golden-yellow veils forming perfect connected circles around each trunk, much like Christmas tree skirts woven together. The sun warmed my wool-covered shoulders despite my making every effort not to move through the shafts of light that peeked through the canopy. The air was rich with the smells of autumn: partially decaying leaves and moist soil predominantly. A nut hatch was upside down on the side of an oak tree at the edge of the swamp. His low pitch honk and periodic, perky and bubbly song was calm and happy. The unalarmed red squirrel was busy gathering acorns. A fisher cat bounded along across my path ahead, clearly determined to get to his den by dusk. I began to think about how much light was left in the day.

I paused just a few feet from my destination, a white oak on a slight knoll. The ledge of rock just under the surface was partially washed away and partly covered by some moss and soil. Not too many dried leaves were here. The tree overlooked a gentle saddle shape in the landscape where I hoped deer would pass through. The area was a partial clearing where a large tree had blown down a couple of years ago. The clear spot was 15 yards wide and 25 yards long, surrounded by open forest and some thin brush. There were indications that deer visited here so my plan was to stay in this tree with my bow until sundown. Standing and surveying the area I would have looked pretty crazy to any human, had anyone been there to see me. I was covered from head to toe in a camouflaged light wool shirt and matching pants. The wool had a slight pile and fuzzy pattern of browns, green and black. My face was blotted and lined with black soot from my wood stove to break up my Caucasian face and ears. I squinted my eyes slightly below the visor of a camouflaged baseball cap. I was scentless except for the hint of deer dander on my boots.

Slowly I opened a glass vile containing a cotton ball with doe urine. I placed the vile at the foot of the tree and began the silent climb. Reaching my perch, I turned carefully to look over the little clearing and forest floor. Suddenly I heard, "CLUNK – rustle, rustle". I looked down to see my deer call had fallen out of my pocket, hit the forest floor and rolled onto the leaves. A bit upset with myself and becoming aware that I needed to settle into this tree soon to prepare for the last of the daylight, I descended the tree with a little less care than usual, shuffling in the leaves as I took a few steps away from the tree to where the deer call rested. Bending over to pick it up, I heard another shuffle in the leaves coming from in front of me and slightly to my right. I froze and listened. I heard it again. I knew I was unmistakably hearing the hooves of an approaching deer. My mind raced. Judging by the sound's volume, this deer had to be within 30 yards of me just beyond the thin brush. Had my stalking, de-scenting and preparation paid off? Apparently so, BUT I was not ready. My arrows were in the quiver and the bow was on my back! And a deer was arriving who clearly did not know a man was in the area. I had managed to get very close to her by coming to my stand quietly. Apparently, she was attracted by the gentle rustle of the leaves when I descended the tree. She was curious to know if she was hearing another deer. She approached cautiously, possibly catching the faint scent of doe urine that I left at the base of the tree. Now she was stepping into the clearing at a cautious but steady pace.

My first thought was to remain frozen to try to avoid being detected. She would clearly see me if I moved when she looked into the clearing. My second thought was "GO for it; you are in a tough set up, but make the best of it." So, I stood slowly to put an arrow on the string and prepared to draw my bow when I had an optimal view of the deer. As the seconds passed and I silently fumbled to get the arrow ready, I stepped onto the mossy spot where the leaves were missing to once again hide my sounds. I adjusted my stance knowing that I would see a snout at any moment. It turned out that there were three does approaching and thankfully at a rate even pokier than I had suspected. Alerted by the faint sounds of leaves and the scent, these three does, with the most mature one in front, began to be partly visible as they inched their way to this little clearing. The lead doe became visible and quartered toward me at a range of only 20 feet! Now that I was sure of my target, I drew my bow as subtly as I could, thinking that at any moment she would realize this was a set up. She gazed into the clearing and scanned the area. I froze at full draw, with my pounding heart the only thing moving. I was sure that she could hear it. The heartbeat throbbed in my ears, and I could feel it pulsing hard in my chest and neck.

I was standing three feet from the base of the tree, apparently looking much like a strangely wide sapling to her. She was clearly surprised not to see another deer right here. After a moment, she took a few steps forward followed by her friends. With her nose alternating systematically from the ground to the air, she was convinced that a deer should be present in the clearing. She scanned the area again, passing her gaze through my body and continuing as though I was part of the landscape. My left arm began to quiver as the muscles rebelled against being asked to hold the draw of the bow for so long. My right hand sweated while holding the release aid which was not secured properly to my wrist due to the lack of preparation time. My trembling arm and breathing felt impossible to conceal at this range.

By now the doe had moved to within 8 feet of me and was facing me head on! But I could not shoot unless she turned to present me her heart. The other does were not presenting feasible targets either.

My focus was on the lead doe because she was the largest. I wonder if she began to suspect that something was not right with the odd tree before her and the strong scent of doe urine without an apparent deer. She was not yet alarmed. The other deer did not detect me either. Nevertheless, with that many sets of deer senses in one area, I knew my time was short. All three deer were still quite fooled at that very short range by my squinted eyes and sooty makeup. The mature doe decided to turn and continue exploring the area. My moment had come and not too soon. My sight pin, dancing due to muscle tremors, found her vital area, and I made a last effort to steady myself before the release. Even at this ridiculously close range, I could not count on the arrow passing through the brisket or the shoulder bone. A broadside shot was all I was willing to take. After what felt like an eternity, my right eye locked onto the deer broadside, and I placed the quivering site pin over her heart. Muscles at their limit, I released the arrow. Fwap! The arrow passed through her and buried itself in the earth not far behind her. Startled by the noise, she jumped a few feet away and looked around to determine what happened. The two other deer also jumped and circled right back. Then the lead deer took three paces more and fell down dead. I was thrilled. The death was painless and quick. The two younger deer eventually moved on, highly suspicious of the funny-shaped tree on the side of the clearing holding a bow. I couldn't take it anymore. I relaxed and lowered the bow, rolling my shoulders to release the tension. This caused the two living deer to bolt away, stopping at a substantial distance just in case their friend was going to follow them.

God surely had orchestrated a big success for me in this situation. I have had good results many times before and since, but never have I experienced all the dimensions of camouflage working so perfectly together. I wish I could say that I could be so stealthy all the time. In reality, such effective use of camouflage is rare. By failing to conceal myself many times I have accrued countless stories of deer snorting and stomping "alarm" before I had even seen them. I would turn to see their white tails high in the air as they bounded away. For me, the hunt chronicled above was an achievement like no other.

Mastery of camouflage will be critical to your success as a hunter. We will examine each of its four dimensions in detail in the next few chapters. Camouflage is primarily about concealment, and in some cases, impersonation. So think of camouflage as duping the senses of the deer by blending with the surroundings as well as by creating artificial sounds, scents and even visual decoys. Fundamentally there has to be a tactic for overriding each of the deer's senses except taste. Therefore the human attributes that we must disguise are: scent, movement, sound and appearance. Let's take a look at each one.

# 5

# Oh My Gosh! You STINK!
## (Scent Control)

*A* deer's primary sense is olfactory. For those of us not in the medical field, that is the sense of smell. If you have a cat, dog or other mammal for a pet at home, you probably have noticed that they use their noses for numerous purposes: to identify people, to determine a good nap spot, to check out the contents of the food bowl. And that is certainly only a partial list. Similarly, deer are very aware of the complete range of normal scents in their woodland home. If an unusual smell is detected in the area, they will respond in proportion to the strength and type of scent. One scent that will put a deer on alert will be that of a predator. Humans not only tend to smell like predators because of the foods we eat but also because we carry a whole host of unusual scents that do not occur in the deer's natural habitat. Because the human sense of smell is so weak compared to the deer's sense of smell, we don't realize how easily we pick up and carry the scent of the "human world" around us. Because deer can "smell us coming" from so far away, we have no idea how often they have effectively avoided us and remained hidden.

Frankly, humans are pretty stinky. Our bodies generate a substantial amount of scent that we don't even notice. This makes it nearly impossible for us to gain close proximity to deer. Even if the wind is carrying our scent away from where we hope the deer are located, our odds of success are severely limited. So we must get rid of our human "body scent". I use the word "human scent" as a broader term to include "body scent" and also any scent not natural to the deer's environment that we carry into the forest. What follows is an exaggerated hypothetical example of how subtle odors are accumulated by one man in about twelve hours.

Jim went to bed after enjoying a wonderful late dinner of steak, garlic-laced mashed potatoes and a glass of red wine. After a good night sleep, Jim woke up in the morning and took a shower. Next, he shaved, got dressed, and had bacon and eggs for breakfast. Then Jim combed his hair, brushed his teeth, and dropped some dog food into the dog's bowl. He patted Butch on the head, grabbed his windbreaker and drove off to work. One the way to work he filled his gas tank at the self-service gas station. Arriving at work, Jim parked his car and looked across the parking lot. He wondered if there were any deer in the little piece of forest behind the office building. Noticing that he was early, he took a minute to walk down the narrow trail leading into the woods to a small clearing about 100 feet in. Now Jim was not good at tracking and did not notice any deer sign. After walking in a bit and looking around he concluded that deer don't visit there. However, what might have happened in this hypothetical story is that there was indeed a herd of deer in the small clearing only minutes earlier.

Of the five deer that vacated the clearing prior to Jim's arrival, one was startled by the unusual "human scent" that he detected. He snorted a warning, sending all the deer bounding away as Jim took his first step off the parking lot and into the woods. Maybe deer number one picked up on the smell of the steak, garlic and red wine on Jim's breath and emanating from his skin. Or maybe it was deer number two who detected the aftershave Jim was wearing, or the drops of bacon grease that fell on his pants during breakfast. Perhaps it was deer number three who did not like the smell of Jim's hair gel, or the food pellets that Jim put in Butch's bowl with his bare hand. Could it have been deer number four who didn't like the smell of cigar smoke on the windbreaker Jim wore when he had stogies with his brother? Or maybe deer number five didn't like the scent of gasoline on Jim's shoes where he stepped into a bit of spilled fuel beside the gas pump.

While a few parts of this story are composites of several scenarios, the overarching point is this: deer are hyper-sensitive to scents that don't typically exist in their habitat. It takes only the faintest whiff of something alien to put them on alert or send them scurrying. The pressure they experience during hunting season further reduces their tolerance for human scent.

There is a process for de-scenting the human body as well as all clothing and gear that will be taken into the forest. Within 24 hours of the hunt, I recommend that you be careful of what you eat. Avoid spicy foods and a lot of red meat. The spices, and to some extent the meat, will change the smell of your breath and skin, so back off on the rich foods the day before you go out to the woods. Alcohol and hunting never mix—for both odor-control and safety reasons. Therefore, I urge you not to drink any beer, wine or hard liquor the day before the hunt. Even a small amount of alcohol will cause you to reek, and there is almost nothing that will clean or cover that scent overnight. If you smoke or even just enjoy an occasional cigar, give it up for the entire hunting season. The only way to remove tobacco scent completely is to take a shower and wash your clothes. Airing out clothes tainted with cigar or cigarette smoke will take too long. In contrast to tobacco, wood fire smoke can actually serve as a cover scent. This will be discussed later.

Proper scent-free laundering/drying of towels and hunting clothes should also take place in advance of hunting day. After drying, these items need to be kept from picking up "human scent". Ideally it is best to have a set of clothes that are reserved for hunting only. I understand that this is not always practical but it is the most effective way to avoid the re-absorption of subtle human odors. Modern hunting attire crafted from quality high-tech fabrics is expensive, especially if designed for cold weather. But for the serious outdoorsman it is worth the investment. With conscientious care, a dedicated hunting outfit that includes long underwear, layers, coat, boots, hat and gloves will serve you well for a very long time.

Whether you have a separate hunting outfit or not, you must follow appropriate procedures for scent-free laundering and drying. You cannot use typical laundry products because they infuse fabrics with a noticeable bouquet. Additionally, there are chemicals in some detergents that will brighten colors and increase the light levels reflected from your clothes into the ultraviolet spectrum. You want to be drab in the woods, not shiny!

There are numerous types of specialized de-scenting laundry soaps available through sportsman retailers and online catalogs. Each brand I have tried has worked well. Most employ oxidizers that react with organic compounds such as hydrocarbons, body oils, and bacteria. The reaction turns these organic compounds into salts. Salt is non-volatile, which means it does not turn into a vapor or gas. Therefore it has no scent. Some products also utilize an aluminosilicate agent, a compound that has a microscopic structure similar to baking soda. Don't worry, you don't need to be a chemist. Just follow the washing instructions on the bottle of hunter's detergent. Be sure to include a towel in the laundry load in order to dry yourself after a "hunter's shower" (explained in an upcoming paragraph). In a pinch, if you cannot get your hands on some hunter's laundry soap before your next visit to the woods, you can put a ½ cup of baking soda into a full wash load to achieve similar odor-removing and antibacterial results. Baking soda raises the ph level of the water which inhibits bacteria growth. The waste products of bacteria create human body odor, so eliminating bacteria will eliminate part of our natural scent. Baking soda can also be applied directly to dry clothes. It consists of tiny crystals with many microscopic caverns that trap scent molecules. Some de-scenting sprays contain baking soda. When sprayed on clothing, the liquid component quickly evaporates leaving soda crystals in the fabric to absorb odors. I will discuss these sprays in more detail later.

Scent-free laundering must be followed by careful drying. If possible, let everything drip dry in an area where there is fresh air. Outside is ideal but indoors is fine as long as the area is free of any prominent scents. If you prefer to use a clothes dryer, be sure not to add a typical dryer sheet! Invariably they are full of perfumes. In fact you might notice that the dryer's interior has retained fragrances accrued from past fabric softener sheets. There are hunter dryer sheets that smell like acorns or dirt but I think their scent is way too strong. I always drip dry my hunting clothes. After the clothes are dry, fold them up and store them in a clean container like a large shipping box, unscented trash bag, dedicated drawer or even a scent-free closet. If you like, hang them outside the day before you use them to freshen them up.

There are several other attire de-scenting options available to us hunters. . . some of those options may seem unusual. If you look in any outfitter's catalog, you will find a myriad of charcoal-filtered boxes, specialty bags, carbon-filled clothing and cover scents. It very likely is all good stuff but I have found that to get the most for your money, using a hunter's laundry soap and a de-scenting spray will get you all the results you need. Feel free to experiment with the other methods out there and use what works best for you.

When hunting day arrives you must take a special shower to get clean and de-scented. For some of us that is a bigger job than others! But rest assured, there are strong soaps out there for our feet, under-arms and other such places. Any sport shop that has hunting products will carry a wide variety of hunter's soap, shampoo and deodorant. Pick up all three. When you shower, make a point of being careful to soap up every bit of skin. You know where you need to clean the most thoroughly so I don't need to go into it. But let me encourage you to be sure to lather every square inch of your body. Scent really can come from anywhere. To dry off, use the towel from the de-scented laundry load described earlier. Next, put on your hunter's deodorant. Don't take these hygiene steps lightly. It is critical that you do not use any common shampoo, conditioner, soap, typical deodorant, or even foot sprays. All this stuff is pungent! I can detect these scents on people from across a parking lot. In fact, sometimes I wonder if deer think that all female humans smell like flowers!

I have been asked what I think of carbon-filled clothing designed to trap odors passing through the fabric. I am quite sure that it works. Be aware though that these articles of clothing need to have the charcoal activated, then cleaned and reactivated after use. This is not hard to do that but it requires some thought and effort. Even if the carbon-filled clothing is 100% effective, the reality is that scents can also travel past the boundaries of our collars, cuffs and open zipper fronts. So charcoal clothing may be a good idea, but it will not replace the proper cleaning of our bodies.

De-scenting sprays are convenient products and can be used on all your gear: your bow, gun, clothing, and the interior and exterior of your hat and boots. Pay special attention to your boots. They are made primarily of leather and rubber—natural materials that tend to stink. I will hang a pair of boots outside for a week or so before hunting season to air them out. If they are brand new, they should probably air out for a month! De-scenting sprays should be used on both the inside and outside of the boot. Just be sure to let them dry out before you put your feet in them. Avoid spraying optics on your gun or bow with de-scenting spray because it leaves a powdery residue.

Guns tend to host a lot of solvent and oil smells if not prepared properly. If you are wise, you will have practiced quite a bit at the range before the opening of hunting season. Then you will clean your guns. Good! But try to clean them far enough in advance of the season so that any volatile liquid residue that remains after cleaning will have a chance to evaporate completely. This evaporation window is necessary because even the most meticulous wiping of firearm parts does not immediately guarantee a residue-free, odor-free gun. There is an old saying that asserts, "It is bad luck to clean your gun the day before a hunt." I don't think luck has anything to do with this apparent truth. I believe all the guys who clean their guns the day before the hunt carry the strong smell of petroleum with them into the woods, which means they'll come out of the woods without venison.

There are low-scent lubricants on the market that you can use for optimal firearm maintenance. However after I have cleaned and oiled my gun, I find it best to wipe away as much of the lubricant as possible. Check with your firearms manual to see if this is acceptable for your gun. For some models it won't be. But I have never had a problem with operating a gun "dry" in the field. The amount of action that the mechanics of your gun will cycle through during a deer hunt is minimal. When we practice with our gun at the range we operate it over and over, going through many rounds of ammunition and sometimes hundreds of mechanical cycles. That activity requires adequate lubrication. But let's face it; a typical hunt in the woods often does not result in a shot at all. I don't wish to be discouraging, just realistic. Most likely you will load the gun at the beginning of the hunt and then unload it at the end of the day, which does not involve much wear. If you are fortunate to take a few shots during the hunt, your gun will still be all right without having to be oiled extensively. Operating it dry for hunting not only reduces scent dramatically, but also eliminates the freezing of your gun in extremely cold environments. Even if the recommended amount of oil does not freeze in your gun's action, it can thicken in the cold and slow down the action enough so that rounds will not feed properly.

Now many gun enthusiasts will argue that a gun should be oiled always! I am not saying it should not be oiled; I am saying that as much oil as possible should be wiped off, and solvents should be given time to evaporate to achieve odor-free dryness. For those of you who are uncomfortable with a dry gun, seek out lubricants that are Teflon-impregnated or marked as low scent. There are synthetic low scent oils available that work well in freezing temperatures. Personally I like Militec™ gun oil for the range. But when I hunt. . . how dry I am.

At last you are ready for the woods because you have eliminated 100% of your scent, right? Well, no. We can't get rid of it all. And our scent will slowly increase during the hunt as we produce new body oils, perspire, and fluff off dander and all the other things shed by mammals. But we have done a great job of cutting our scent way down. Even if a deer's nose does detect us, he is likely to misjudge our distance and think we are far away instead of close by. But let us not be satisfied with that. To help us get even closer to our prey I will introduce the use of "cover scent".

In the early days, when hot water and soap were not as readily accessible, people endured chronic unpleasant body odor. Eventually they found that putting on perfume was a good solution because its flowery aroma was usually strong enough to mask their offensive body odor. These resourceful folks were using a form of "cover scent." We are going to employ a similar tactic for hunting. Note the word similar. I have seen more hunters get the use of cover scent all wrong. In fact I believe that more than half of cover scent practitioners actually reduce their success by the way they foolishly overdo this tactic. The idea is to be subtle, and I want to emphasize the word subtle. Our goal is to mask our already greatly-reduced odor without raising deer awareness of the cover scent. I want to state that again: a cover scent should go unnoticed by the deer! Think of cover scent as part of your camouflage. It should not call attention to itself. It should blend naturally with other forest smells. A successful, unnoticeable olfactory cover depends on two key factors: the type of the scent, and the strength of the scent.

If we want to camouflage ourselves visually in a pine grove, we would likely choose a dappled green and brown coat. If we are going to hunt in a snow covered forest, we would typically don a white jacket with scattered black or brown patches breaking up its brightness. Both of these camouflage patterns would not be a good choice for hiding in an inflatable bouncy house of red balls. In that case, one might choose a red shirt. The same thinking is necessary when choosing a cover scent. To select the right cover scent, examine your hunting environment. What scents occur there naturally? Are you in pines or oaks? Is the ground dirt or swamp? By rubbing pine needles on your boots while hunting in a pine grove, or by grinding your boots in swamp mud while hunting on the edge of the swamp, you have covered one of your greatest scent liabilities—your boots and feet. Furthermore, you have acquired a scent that is naturally occurring in that location. The scent should be weak. If you can smell it, you are probably using too much.

Sometimes you may need to generate several cover scents in one day if you hunt in multiple areas. For example, while preparing to hunt on the edge of an apple orchard, you decide to crush an apple against each boot. Good plan. But in the afternoon, when you go back to the pine grove miles from the orchard, it may make a deer a bit more alert when he gets a snout full of apple scent as he approaches his beloved pine bed. He may not startle but he will become more aware of an unusual scent as he approaches. We don't want the deer looking around trying to find the source of the unusual scent. We don't want the deer to be on alert at all. They are already difficult to fool. If you don't think the cover scent is right, it is best not to use one.

One guy I know puts on skunk odor where he hunts. He insists it has worked for him one time. I was surprised to find the product on the shelf of a sports shop. Well, I don't think deer are thrilled to come into an area that has the heavy scent of skunk in it. A deer may not detect the "human scent" in the area, but he's going to be wondering: "What the heck happened here to upset that skunk?" And his eyes are going to be scanning for the source of that scent. So pick an innocuous scent like acorn, pine, earth or even grass if it is local. The key word in that idea is local—something that will blend naturally with the smells in that habitat. And I'll say it one more time, if you can smell the cover scent on your own body, it is likely more than you need.

A large percentage of homes in my neighborhood heat their homes with wood stoves when autumn's chill arrives. Therefore the region's deer have become familiar with and comfortable around the scent of wood smoke. If this is the case for you too, you might consider letting some smoke cling to your boots or jacket. Just wave your jacket over your campfire once or twice and you are all set.

Don't overdo it or you will hit the woods smelling like a forest fire. Remember, you are de-scented almost completely and will need only a light cover.

Now that the scent from our body and clothing is under control, we must be careful not to contaminate ourselves with unwanted odors on our way in to the hunt. Pay close attention to routine habits or actions that could accidently restore smells from your human surroundings. On your way to the forest, never pump gasoline into your vehicle. Gasoline or diesel fumes on your shoes, hands or clothes are so strong and unnatural you may as well walk into the forest blowing an air horn. Don't even check your tire pressure. Rubber can carry a strong petroleum scent. There are many other more subtle scents we can acquire unknowingly. If my wife is making chili or cooking fish, I will not pass through the kitchen on my way out to the woods. Our hair and clothing are scent traps and dispensers. Keep your head covered with a hat when possible to avoid picking up or dispensing too much scent. Some guys don't put their hunting clothes on until they arrive at the forest. They keep the de-scented attire in a bag and change after they get out of their car. Then they head into the woods. While this is not my preference, it is a good option.

As we enter the forest de-scented enough to prevent deer from detecting us and running away, is there anything we can do to attract them? Yes, bucks and does are naturally drawn to certain scents. Sometimes I like to use a deer scent lure. This is a tricky thing but well worth trying once in a while. I don't recommend using scent lures all the time because they are designed to change deer behavior. It is wise to learn natural deer behavior first, and set up a hunt accordingly. Then it can be fun and rewarding to attract deer to an area by using scent lures as well. Choosing the right one can be more art than science and we won't be able to examine every scenario. Also note as I said before, that an unusual scent will heighten a deer's awareness and raise your chances of being detected. Sometimes it is worth the risk. Here are a few ideas for attracting your prey:

If you are interested in harvesting a deer of either sex, and the rut has not started, try food scents. These can be made at home or purchased at your favorite outfitter. Some good food scents are white oak acorn, apple cider, molasses and peanut butter. Soak a clean rag in apple cider and lay it over a down wind branch within comfortable shooting range. A deer attracted by the scent will not be drawn directly to you. Place the scent dispenser at the animal's approximate nose height or lower. While walking, deer tend to have their head down low to the ground or straight out from their shoulders.

That is often about knee to hip height on a human. Now you have a set up that will bring the deer to your optimal spot for a clear shot.

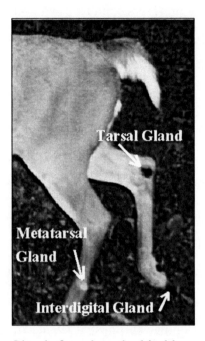

Glands found on the hind legs

There are other scent lure types that take advantage of a deer's curious nature. Tarsal scent, anise scent (licorice) and non-estrous urine are innocuous smells that will bring a deer into an area to investigate their source. Tarsal scent (from the rear leg joint, much like the heel or reverse facing knee), metatarsal scent (from a gland a few inches above the hoof) and interdigital scent (from a gland in the clove of the hoof) are often dispensed strongly as a result of a deer stomping the ground. Deer tend to stomp when they sense danger or when they are trying to encourage a predator to move or show itself. Deer that have suspected my presence in their terrain have often stomped the ground. This behavior might also communicate concern to other bucks & does. Tarsal scent glands are located on the inside of the rear legs of the deer where the fur is a bit longer and darker. When relieving itself, a deer will often mix secretions from this gland with urine. It is a complicated scent type that I rarely use because too much of it can actually scare away deer. Nevertheless, many people utilize it successfully. My personal favorite in this category of scent lures is simply the urine itself, the "doe pee." It will prompt curious deer of both sexes and all ages to find out who the "newcomer" is. I have lost count of how many deer have approached my area looking for the source of that scent. Best of all, they come in relaxed because the scent is common and not alarming.

During the rut and the week leading up to the rut, you might use a sexual attractant. Now sexual attractants can have some funny effects making them a bit more challenging to use than curiosity scents. But when the conditions are right, they will yield a super response. If the does are in heat, rutting bucks will find doe estrous scent lures practically irresistible. Sometimes does will also be drawn to estrous scent out of curiosity. However, does who are not in heat try to avoid being harassed by bucks seeking out receptive females. Until they too are ready to mate, these ladies will usually stay clear of a doe in heat and her scent. Keep this in mind if you have a doe tag in your possession. If you are seeking to fill that tag, the use of estrous urine is not your best option. But if you are interested in shooting a buck, this scent can make for an exciting day!

As I indicated earlier, bucks are typically more wary and more careful than does. But give them a whiff of estrous scent and there will be a potent response coupled with the tendency to be a bit less guarded. A buck's sexual drive is so powerful that he will seek out and tend to does in heat, even to the point of causing himself harm such as exhaustion or starvation. But there is a wide spectrum of buck personalities. The most cautious buck will note the area where he detected the scent and return at night to investigate, when the hunters are not in the woods. Others will enter the location with their radar on full alert. Don't be careless during rutting season because bucks almost always approach a spot looking, sniffing and listening for the slightest clues about another's presence. Sometimes you might encounter a fool hardy buck, usually an immature one. He will have such a case of raging hormones that he will run into the area with the fur on his back and neck standing up like the fur on a frightened cat, except that he's not afraid, he's on a mission. He might gallop right up to your lure and suddenly stop where the scent is strongest. He'll swing his head left and right looking for the doe and even grunt as if to say, "Hey! Where are you??" It is quite a thing to see, and even though I find it humorous, I never laugh. When the bucks come in like that, it is exciting and time to make the shot. . . I'm all business. Estrous scent will be effective roughly a week or so before the rut and only slightly effective post rut. If the rut is not on, this scent's effect will be similar to regular deer urine. Do remember these are general rules. Don't hesitate to experiment.

Dominant buck urine is another scent lure that I have tried. You can read stories published in outdoorsman magazines by professional hunters who achieved good results with this lure. My experience with dominant buck urine has been so mixed that I hesitate to recommend it. The purpose of this scent is to evoke a territorial response from the bucks in the area, causing them to appear and face the "challenger" in defense of their turf. While the expectations for this scent seem feasible, I believe it can sometimes backfire in practice: if a buck with a non-confrontational personality gets a whiff of this monster buck urine, he may just avoid the supposedly dominant male. That "male" is you. His behavior does not make him a wimpy buck. He may very well be a huge, mature fella with an impressive antler rack on his head. He attained that stature because he was careful about picking his battles. You will need a different strategy to bag him someday. If the lure is working as anticipated, you may attract a big bruiser who's looking for a fight and will boldly step right into your line-of-sight. This scent is considered most effective in the pre-rut and partly so during the rut. Some say it can lure does, however I cannot confirm that because I have never seen a doe investigate dominant buck urine. Experiment with it if you wish. It is low on my list of tools.

I will close out this discussion of scent lures with tips on how to dispense scent for optimum effectiveness. There are various wicks—available at most hunting stores—that are designed to soak up scents such as urine, and aid in the vaporization. However, if you want to make your own, you can cut a piece of clean cotton fabric from an old t-shirt. Be sure to clean it well. Cotton makes an excellent scent wick because it is highly absorbent and readily available. Cut your fabric into 4x4 inch squares. Before heading out to hunt, place one square in a sandwich baggie, add some liquid scent, and seal the baggie. When you arrive at your hunting location, simply take out the piece of stinky fabric, and lay it over a log or low branch. To be most realistic, the wick should be placed at the approximate height of an adult deer's rear end. I have seen hunters hang these scent wicks at eye level for a six foot tall man. That is not natural, and most of the scent will waft above a deer's head. Air movement will disperse scent vapor at any height, so I am not saying that the scent wick position is ultra-critical. Some guys insist on placing the lure at a deer's nose height only. I have observed that a deer's nose moves up and down quite a bit during travel. When standing still, deer often put their noses to the ground and rarely pose with their heads held high. At other times a deer's nose hovers just above its belly. Because the altitude of the scent dispenser is not crucial you can determine a placement height that makes sense for the surroundings. There is just one caveat: avoid putting the wick on a rock. Rocks draw the heat out of everything, and cold wicks do not efficiently dispense scent.

Earlier we talked about wearing cover scent to help camouflage our human odors. But unlike these odor masks, scent lures should never be worn on your body. We don't want to attract the deer to our exact position. We want to draw them to a good shooting lane. This is why a scent lure should be placed at a comfortable shooting distance and in a direction that is generally downwind from your position, as I mentioned previously. Contrary to the popular notion reinforced by hunting magazine articles, deer do not always come into the scent from downwind. Think about it. If deer only walked with the wind in their faces, they would eventually all congregate on one side of the forest and reside there until the weather pattern changed. Deer will travel in any direction they wish, including into the wind when necessary for an olfactory advantage. Therefore it is a good idea to put out multiple scent wicks each at a distance that you can accurately make a shot.

To draw deer in along a scent trail, tie one end of a three or four-foot length of string to one of your homemade scent lures; tie the other end to your boot. Walk carefully. I have tripped myself doing this. Drag the scent rag behind you and trace a giant "figure eight" on the ground formed by two approximately 100-yard-diameter circles. Leave the scent lure at the intersection of the "figure eight". Place yourself at a comfortable shooting distance from the intersection and wait. Any deer crossing the scent trail should eventually come to your lure!

This wraps up the hunter's guide to scent control. Some folks take this aspect of hunting quite seriously; others don't even bother with it. I know one guy who smokes cigarettes while hunting, and it's not surprising that there are many years during which he fails to bag a deer. Other outdoorsmen insist: "You have to play the wind," as the old saying goes. I don't want to belittle that idea, but I cannot control the wind nor constantly keep track of its shifting speeds and fickle changes-of-direction. By contrast, some people are such perfectionists about scent control that they don't put on their odor-free hunting clothes until they arrive at the forest edge, even in the coldest, wettest weather. As I mentioned earlier, I admire their rugged discipline, but I prefer to don de-scented duds at home. I recommend that you do your best to practice scent control without making it a hardship. Remember that scent lures are optional and suited to much experimentation. When combined with careful de-scenting—and basic knowledge of tracking and deer behavior—attractants can increase your odds of success. If you apply what you have read in this chapter, you will experience good results. It is a thrill to dupe a deer's sense of smell!

# James Bond
# Or Maxwell Smart?
## (How To Camouflage Your Movement)

*W*e spoke about "full field" vision in Chapter Four. Although it would be difficult to prove scientifically, I believe that most wild animals use their full field of vision. Please recall that "full field" vision results in a high sensitivity to movement. So it becomes a challenge to the hunter to avoid being detected by deer because of man's natural need to move and the animal's superior ability to notice his motion. If you are new to hunting you will be amazed by how deer can pick up on your smallest movements and lock eyes with you instantly. Then when you gulp or blink, they will raise their tails and bound away, disappearing into the woods. I am intentionally writing about how to camouflage human movement before writing about how to camouflage human appearance because I believe the former is more important for a successful hunt. I have hidden from people and animals while I was wearing blue jeans and a bright red shirt just by standing still. This proved to me first hand that camouflaging movement is essential. Of course we do have to move about in the forest during part of the hunt, so let's learn five effective techniques for minimizing detection: posturing, mirroring the environment, taking advantage of visual dead zones, covering movement and being willing to slow down.

"Posturing" refers to how we position our bodies during the hunt. The term includes stalking. When outdoors, humans spend much of their time upright. Animals in most habitats are accustomed to seeing people in this vertical position and can easily identify human visitors. Therefore, merely changing our body shape will substantially conceal our movements.

One sunny afternoon I had the pleasure of watching several deer grazing because I had taken a rest against a tree to read a book. My whole body was lying on the grass, and my head was raised slightly against the base of the tree. The deer that came to the field to graze eventually noticed the strange form leaning on the trunk. I flipped pages as I read moving my hands normally. But the deer did not spook right away. In fact, they were curious and came closer. I looked unusual, not threatening and certainly not human. It took them awhile to identify me. They eventually did because they picked up on my scent. But until that happened they were not sure what I was. All I had done to become "approachable" was to change my posture by lying down. I did not even need to be perfectly still to appear nonthreatening. Deer rarely, if ever, see people in a posture other than standing up straight. So keep in mind that you can take advantage of this fact. Deer hunting is a good time to practice bad posture.

There are numerous ways a person can stalk, crawl and snake his body to avoid detection by woodland creatures, but it is not necessary to get too extreme while hunting. I enjoyed a survival class many years ago where we learned some crazy ways of moving that I think had more application to military operations than to whitetail deer hunting. One technique involved a caterpillar movement while lying on my belly. It was difficult and slow, and I ended up with blisters on my chest. However, I was impressed with how well it worked. Even so, I have never used it hunting. Instead I want to talk about basic stalking movements. Skillful stalking takes a tremendous amount of strength, balance and practice. To do it well you need to be physically fit because stalking is quite different from walking. You will exert much physical energy making demands on little-used muscles, and you will expend much mental energy sustaining awareness and balance.

Why is stalking more demanding than ordinary walking? Modern civilizations have been away from "rugged frontier living" for so long that our brains have reprogrammed how we walk. Our improved construction standards have provided level floors and sidewalks that enable us to amble on perfect horizontal planes most of the time. And modern stairs are so uniform that we can safely ascend and descend without thinking about it, even in the dark. As a result, our gait has become very regular. Additionally, we seldom need to be quiet within our communities, so our feet tend to make a lot of noise flopping, shuffling and pounding on indoor and outdoor surfaces. Our purpose for walking is almost always a simple process of getting from point A to point B. Our steps form a low-energy, relaxed gait that displays a rolling heel-to-toe movement. Our legs extend in front of us, shifting our weight—our center of gravity—slightly beyond our bodies. Consequently, we are always "falling forward" as our legs continually step ahead, saving us from falling down. I am sure that sounds strange. However, the truth of this becomes very evident the first time a person attempts to walk through the woods.

Novices in the forest are easy to spot. As soon as they start out on a hike, they will likely stub their toes on the undulating terrain of roots, rocks, sticks and other natural clutter. Their feet kick through debris and trudge noisily through leaves. Twigs snap under foot, reminding these folks of the risk of falling and breaking an ankle. Unhappy with the performance of their legs and feet, the individuals change their hiking method. First they drop their heads and look at the ground directly ahead of their feet as they walk. Now they will not stumble, but they will probably still tramp loudly and walk heel-to-toe. Without further instruction, most forest visitors will never improve their sylvan ambulatory skills beyond this awkward habit. There is no harm in it really, except that while they are safely propelling themselves forward, they cannot observe their surroundings because their heads are down. To view the sights they must stop, stand still, and look around. This pattern just does not lend itself well to hunting! Not only are the individuals not seeing what is around them until they stop walking, but they are also scaring away any animals that may have been in the area long before these noisy folks came within visual range. Even I can hear people traipsing through the forest when they are still a long way off, because human footsteps are distinct from those of any other creature. All the animals know this. If I can detect distant people in the woods, just imagine how easily animals can with their keener hearing!

Now I will share with you two techniques that camouflage the hunter's unique human movement: the "half stalk" and the "full stalk". The "half stalk" mimics the way predators such as foxes, cats, and other diagonal walkers sneak up on their prey. Diagonal walkers are animals that lift the left front paw and right rear paw simultaneously as they move forward, followed by lifting the right front paw and left rear paw together. The "half stalk" is a low noise, high awareness movement that only slightly obscures our posture and limbs, and is not too strenuous.

Begin by bending your knees slightly and keeping them bent at all times. Keep your upper body straight and your eyes slightly below straight ahead. Use your "full field" vision to see everything in front of you, above you, left and right, as well as where your front foot is going to land. Granted, you will have only a partial view of where your foot will land, but that is sufficient. You want the majority of your visual awareness up and ahead. Your feet will "feel" the ground as you step, and constantly transmit information to your brain about twigs, brush, rocks and undulating earth below your field-of-vision.

This brings up the type of shoe you wear. Obviously, bare feet work best for feeling the ground. But we have to be realistic. On gentle terrain, thin-soled shoes such as moccasins and boat loafers provide light protection with little reduction in tactile sensitivity. For tougher hunting conditions you need more rugged footwear. Most hunters wear hiking boots in fair weather and heavy insulated boots for cold and wet weather. With time, you will learn to feel the ground with boots on. Your feet will be much less sensitive through thick soles, but they will still be able to detect twigs that might snap, tangles and uneven surfaces.

When you are steadily balanced, lift one knee almost level with your hip and point your toe down. Slowly lower your pointed toe toward the ground, through blueberry bushes or other low plant life, and aim it about 12 inches ahead of your rear foot. Continue lowering the toe until it touches the ground. Keep your eyes ahead and see everything. Feel the terrain with your toe and then with the ball of your foot to determine what is beneath. No stick to snap? Good. Press down gradually on the ball of your foot and roll your weight to the outer edge. Then slowly lower the heel, feeling all the time, and being careful not to make excessive noise. With both feet planted, cautiously shift your weight to the front foot and lift your rear foot so that your knee rises almost level with your hip again. Then repeat the descent like your front foot did earlier: with toes down, lower your pointed foot through the brush and toward the forest floor. The movement is a cycle of lifting the knee high, pointing the toe down, touching the forest floor, feeling with the toe, rolling to the ball, rolling to the outer edge, settling the heel, adding weight.

In the next cycle, raise your knee and FREEZE! Make a point of keeping your center of balance over your feet at all times. You will know that you are controlling your weight well by being able to freeze perfectly still at any point during your half stalk and not fall down. This is essential when you detect game and want to stop moving immediately, or if you accidently snap a twig and need to freeze briefly until the forest settles down again. Take a few minutes now to try a couple of half stalk steps. How do your legs feel? Are they burning a bit? They very likely will!

This high stepping will eventually feel natural and will make a lot of sense on uneven forest floors covered in brush and debris. As you practice, you will become skilled enough to stop using your arms for balance. Yes, I know you have been using them to help you remain upright. Now put your arms straight down by your sides, or fold your hands together at your belly button. If you are a bow hunter, you will have your bow in your non-dominant hand and against your chest for this stalk. Your dominant hand will likely be clutching an arrow or be nestled in your pocket. If you are a gun hunter, it is best to cradle your gun with your non-dominant hand behind the trigger guard, and lean the muzzle into the crook of your elbow of the same arm. This is a very comfortable and safe position. Always remember that your hands and arms are not to move at all when you are stalking. Your elbows should be braced firmly against your body. After all, what animal walks upright and has long dangly limbs? Your arms are part of what makes you look human. Hide them.

If you practice this half stalk prior to the next hunting trip, you will become stronger, quieter and stealthier. This will enhance your likelihood of seeing animals before they see you, and you might just get very close to them. Personally, I do this stalk 90% of the time that I am moving during a hunt. This is not to say that I don't "walk" in the woods. But generally, the half stalk is the movement that I use most.

The "full stalk" is employed when you are trying to move through an area in which deer and other animals are surely present, or when you do not want to cause even the slightest disturbance. Remember, even if the deer does not see you, the red squirrel or blue jay might notice and scold you, thus alerting the deer to your approach. The full stalk enables you to hide from everything, including the "tattle-tales." It is the same as the half stalk except much slower and more difficult to sustain for a long time. Curl your back over so that your knees almost reach your chest as you walk. Next, your legs and feet should perform the same movements used for the half stalk. Although your back is curled forward or hunched, you still must keep your head looking forward. In this position you will see less of where your feet land because your head is now the leading part of your body. However, your shape will no longer look human. If you are spotted, you will be a couple of feet shorter and resemble an animal, which will make you less likely to scare away other creatures. This position lends itself to hiding behind low brush. During practice, place your hands on each knee and keep your elbows against your ribs. This will help support your upper body and relieve lower back fatigue. During the hunt you will be carrying a bow or gun. Your weapon can be carried in your non-dominant hand, under your chest, or if you prefer, it can hang from your arms as they point straight down. Personally I prefer the weapon tucked in front of me.

Just as with the half stalk, the key to success in the full stalk is to keep your balance perfect so that you can freeze and hold your position at any point in the movement. Your eyes and ears should be full field and unfiltered respectively. Feel with your feet. Roll your feet down: toe, ball and side, then the heel. Move as slowly as you can comfortably. Increase your speed only if there is both visual and audible cover such as brush to hide behind or wind to mask your noise. Try not to think about the time it takes to travel. Be patient. Stalking practice and perseverance will eventually reap great rewards.

As I mentioned earlier in this chapter, there is another side to camouflaging one's movement. It is to "mirror the environment". As a child, did you and a friend ever play "Mirror?" In that game, two people face each other. Then one moves his hands and makes faces while the other imitates those same actions just like a mirror reflection. When I was a kid I played that game. It comes to mind whenever I think about making my movements mirror the environment. Mimicking the motions of the forest can be simple or challenging, and sometimes it just isn't possible. The following is an anecdotal look at how to camouflage movement by mirroring the forest:

Making your way into your favorite hunting ground, you pass though a piece of forest toward a field where you hope to spot deer before sundown. There is a very good chance they are in the field already or they may be just on the edge of the forest on the other side. Uncertain about where the deer are, you shift into a "full stalk" and move super slowly through an oak grove. Your ears pick up the faintest of sounds from the forest. All is very still, and with your micro-pace you more closely resemble a tree stump than anything animate. Each step is taking about thirty seconds. As you listen, you begin to hear the quiet hiss of the leaves at the top of the oak canopy above as they begin to respond to a breeze aloft. You can't see the motion yet, but the sound level increases as the breeze makes its way down toward the forest floor. Now the lower branches of the oaks and the little saplings next to you begin to sway and flutter. You respond with a faster gait; the noise of your feet is masked by the sound of the wind. Your hunched body bobs and sways slightly, mirroring the motion of the trees around you as you stalk more quickly. Your movements continue to mimic your environment as you pass by. Then you begin to detect the breeze ebbing away. You note the fading sound and observe the more delicate flutter of the leaves. You too begin to slow your gait back down. Your upper body no longer bobs, and you become less kinetic along with the forest. Two more silent steps and you come to rest beside a boulder, holding still, both feet on the ground. Now resembling the boulder, you catch your breath while hunched over and scanning the forest with all your senses. Refreshed, you begin to stalk again, delighted to hear another breeze stirring the leaves and small branches. Your skillful forest imitation just might fool a savvy deer long enough for you to spot him first!

While camouflaging your movement, take advantage of "visual dead zones". A visual dead zone is an area or direction toward which a creature is not looking. The animal might be distracted by something elsewhere, but not always. It can be difficult to find visual dead zones in the woods, yet it is worth mentioning. For example, if you find a game trail that skirts around a grassy yard surrounding a home, you can be pretty sure that deer traversing this trail will turn their attention toward the yard rather than toward the opposite direction. Therefore, if you want to be less conspicuous when hunting here, you should keep the deer trail between you and the yard. The side of a hill can sometimes serve as a visual dead zone because animals tend to scan the tops of hills and the valleys below before they scan the slopes. If there is an exceptionally large pine tree that stands out in the landscape, don't walk directly past it because it probably draws every animal's gaze. Visually sweep the terrain and plan your route through the areas that did not catch your eye. These are not always the easiest paths but they will help you remain inconspicuous and give you a stalking advantage.

You have now learned about some common visual dead zones. But there are countless others that can vary among animals, even within a species, so it is virtually impossible to identify every type. Consider a deer approaching an orchard from the north. If he is relaxed, he will most likely enter the orchard from a game trail. He will slow his pace as he nears the clearing, and inevitably pause for a while near the end of the trail to allow his senses to evaluate the area thoroughly. Where do you think the visual dead zone might be? For a wise old buck there probably won't be any. However, he will most likely scan the center, east and west sides carefully. Then if all is well, he may scan the far south side. If satisfied, he will move out a short distance into the clearing, put his nose to the ground to pick up any animal traffic scent, and then pick his head up again for another scan. Throughout this process, his visual dead zones are possibly the transition zones just left and right of the trail on the north side, the side from which he approached. I have watched a few deer exhibit this type of blind-spot. Is this a reliable visual dead zone? Absolutely not. Will it vary from deer to deer? Absolutely. But I had one young buck walk right past me at the end of a game trail that opened into an orchard. He was looking for movement in the orchard and not along the end of the trail. On a side note, we humans have frequent "visual dead zones" because we are inclined toward tunnel vision and are not very aware of our surroundings. After all, we don't have to worry much about predators, so we are seldom motivated to pay attention to things beyond our personal space.

Another factor to consider when camouflaging movement is strong sunlight. We often forget that the canopy of branches and leaves above us is not a "solid ceiling." It allows irregular shafts of sunlight to stream through to the forest floor illuminating everything in their paths. As we pass through those shafts, we stand out like a glowing rock star in the spotlight on stage. Though this visual effect is desirable on stage, it is quite detrimental to hunters trying to stay out of sight. No matter how carefully we stalk, these light beams shine and flicker rapidly over our bodies as we move drawing attention. When that happens we might as well place a twirling red fire truck beacon on our heads. While moving through an area, try to avoid these sunny spotlights as well as any larger bright patches. Sometimes it is impossible to evade every sunbeam, but whenever you can, creep through shadows and brush that will hide you and obscure your movements. Take advantage of "cover". When you need to get across a small clearing, don't stalk through the middle no matter how easy and efficient it may be. Choose a route on the shadiest side of the perimeter to maximize your camouflage.

The final motion-camouflaging strategy is to slow down and minimize unconscious, unnecessary movements. For me this is the toughest thing to do. I want to get where I am going quickly. I just have to remember that whenever I am hunting my goal is to bag a deer, not to arrive at a destination. As a result, I often need to remind myself to "slow down". I also need to be aware of my small, superfluous actions that can give away my position. We all have to scratch our noses sometimes. We have to adjust our hats and put on our gloves. Maybe we need to put on one more layer of clothing from our backpacks. Treat these actions as stalking movements. Perform them with minimal activity close to your body, and at a speed that is painfully slow in order to preserve the illusion of stillness. As I mentioned earlier, you will occasionally be observed by other wildlife, especially birds and squirrels that love to sound the alarm about your arrival. Make every effort to hide from everything.

Becoming a skilled stalker is one of the greatest challenges for hunters. Most don't even try to traverse the forest undetected. I've seen many outdoorsmen just plod along like Maxwell Smart, heads down on their way to their hunting area, and totally unaware of my presence; consequently they will also be unaware of an animal's presence. Whether you hunt on the move or from a still point, blending into the motion of the habitat will increase your deer sightings and potentially shorten your shooting distance. This is a thrilling and rewarding experience. Practice & patience will make you the "007" of the woods.

 7

# Elmer Fudd
## (What To Do With Sound)

"**S**hhhhh Be vewwy vewwy quiet. . . I'm hunting wabbit! Heh-heh-heh-heh." Good ol' Elmer Fudd. Now there is inspiration! He reminds me to have fun and not take myself too seriously. And what better quote is there to kick off a discussion about the role of sound during a hunt?

Whether one needs to be super quiet or not while hunting rabbit with a shotgun is a debate for another day. It is time to turn our attention back to bigger game, and I have an exciting topic ahead regarding camouflaging sound while whitetail hunting. Sound is one of the toughest things to eliminate, but it is also one of the easiest things to falsify. Often, beginner hunters do not realize the amount of human noise that they make. I'll never forget the day I slipped my way to the edge of a clearing in up-state New York with an acquaintance who didn't hunt. There were deer in this piece of forest and I was hoping to get a look into the clearing to see if we could catch a glimpse of them. My inexperienced companion was about a stone's throw behind me as I peeked through the bushes at the forest's edge.

He yelled at the top of his voice "Hey! Can you see anything? Any deer there?" I thought he was joking with me. It turned out, he was REALLY inexperienced. In this case, sound was a detriment, but it can also work to our advantage. Carefully generated sounds can summon almost any animal and certainly the whitetail deer. These can be mastered with very little practice. In this chapter we will study how to use sound successfully to attract deer. We will also learn to avoid common call-replication goofs.

It was the first Saturday of gun season for deer. Eddie, one of my early hunting buddies, invited me to hunt with him along with another friend of his. We went to an area that I had never visited. Arriving before dawn, we parked the truck. I was a bit surprised when Eddie told me: "Head that way a bit and I'll see ya 'round lunch time." That wasn't the friendliest thing to do. He was a bit rough around the edges, but if he invited me to hunt with him I knew there would be deer. Eddie is a highly-skilled hunter and a dedicated one. He'll steer you toward a spot where deer are plentiful. Nevertheless, it is important to give a newcomer to the forest a bit more information than "go that way", especially when the trek begins before first light.

I headed into this 1000-acre parcel guided by my compass and the delicate light from my headlamp. I soon discovered that this sizable piece of forest had quite a few manmade paths as well as wide fire lanes, which alleviated my concern about getting lost. After walking in a straight line for five minutes, I stood still and waited for first light. Soon I could see. Within a half hour after sunrise I was quite surprised and amused to find the forest filling up with hunters. It was as though everyone and his brother and uncle and aunt showed up. I remember it well. You would not have seen more orange in a Florida citrus grove. Everyone had a shotgun over his shoulder. To add to the oddity of it all, I had taken my bow with me. I said hello to one fellow to help ease the awkwardness of our proximity while hunting. He gave me a funny look, gestured toward my bow, and asked sarcastically "What are you gonna' do with that?" I had to admit I was wondering the same thing at that moment. Bow hunting is great when deer are calm. But the deer would be on edge with this crowd roaming around in their habitat. A gun would have been a better option.

Completely thrown by the human traffic, the unfamiliar forest and my short range bow, I decided it was time to rethink tactics or get the heck out of there. I could not believe that there were so many people tromping through the woods. Being young and a bit optimistic I decided to stay and work out a fitting strategy. . . or so I hoped. Although I had no experience hunting in such a high pressure scenario, I began to think that there might be a way to put all these people to work for me. If my ears and eyes were filled with human stimuli, then the deer surely were even more aware that something was up. There may as well have been a marching band, complete with horns and drum section, coming down the fire lane.

Behind me was a group of five guys covered from head to toe in orange. Their conversation was clear and loud and peppered with laughter. It seemed to me that the average hunter in this plethora of folk was interested only in taking his gun for a walk in the woods. To increase my own odds of success, my bow and I had to get to a tough, unappealing route or area that these less-experienced folks would avoid. Normally deer hide in common areas and even small thickets. But when there is a lot of traffic in the forest, they head for the tough stuff where hunters don't want to go such as swamps, briars, or thick and impenetrable brambles. My plan was to try to find the escape routes and places where the deer might funnel down due to the contours of the land as they headed to their best hiding places—if the entire herd was not already pushed through such spots. This was a big challenge because I was not familiar with this forest at all. I think I had some supernatural help because at the end of the day, the guys I came to the forest with had not seen any deer. I, on the other hand, got to see a herd run through. They were traveling too fast for me to count them. And I didn't even take a shot because a good shot never presented itself. Nevertheless, it worked out pretty well, and I used sound to get close. Here is how I did it.

I was making my way through a hardwood section of forest. The area was open enough for a bow shot. To my right I found dense lowland that I was sure would be a good escape for the deer. Unsure of how they might approach, I slowly moved along this transition from open hardwood to thick, low wetland hoping for a clue. Before long I crossed an obvious deer run. This could be it. There was a narrow path roughly one foot in width where the vegetation and the leaves were clearly trampled. In some spots along the path, the dirt was exposed and the hoof prints were easily visible. I began looking for a place to hide on the other side of the run. As I climbed up a slope, I discovered a saddle where two small hills came together creating a valley about 70 yards long. In the bottom of the valley was a wider and more heavily used deer run. I backed up to assess the area from the top of the knoll, keeping my head down and trying to be stealthy. There were a couple of orange vests directly behind me, but they were walking along a human foot trail unaware of my presence. Then it happened. I heard gun fire to my left from at least 100 or more yards away, followed by the crashing through the forest of many hooves. Before I could attempt to hide and pick a shooting lane through the trees, I nocked an arrow and stared in the direction of what thundered like a stampede. Gambling that they would take the more worn path I prepared for a 25-yard shot. There was no time to try to get closer to the path and be ready with the bow. And I didn't know if they would use that path. So I drew the bow and waited as the herd crashed into view, bolting down the heavily-used highway toward the wetlands. At least a dozen deer went by at nearly a full gallop, weaving through the trees and flashing their tales as they passed. Surprisingly, about five of them stopped to look over their shoulders just slightly left of where I could easily release an arrow. Knowing this was my opportunity, I repositioned to make a shot.

But the deer took off again loping and trotting after the herd, disappearing quickly in the thick forest. I lowered the bow and breathed. My heart was racing. Straining to see where the deer had gone, I once again heard the sound of hooves coming from the left. A straggler! He nervously walked into view, clearly trying to listen for the herd that had passed just moments before while staying ahead of whatever danger he had perceived earlier. His nose dropped to the ground to pick up the scent of the herd but he did not slow down. I was suddenly inspired to stamp my feet to simulate the rhythmic pattern of the herd's pounding hooves. Believe it or not, that young buck turned right and headed straight for me, still hustling along with his nose to the ground. My left shoulder was against a tree for cover. I drew the bow again and prepared for him to pass. And pass he did. . . within five feet of me! He trotted by and headed over the knoll. This deer had actually come off the trail and ascended the knoll following the sound of my boots. I was close enough to step over and spank him. He had truly responded to my mimicking the hooves of other deer on the move. Wow!

I don't think I will ever be confident enough to release an arrow at a deer moving that fast. I hadn't even tried to stop him with another curious sound. Odds are he would not have fully stopped no matter what noise I made until he was well hidden. But I learned a valuable lesson that day: I could use sound to my advantage. I had also successfully carried out a method of handling heavy hunting pressure. Chock up another day of experience in the field.

When trying to be stealthy during a hunt, you want to avoid making any distinctly human sounds. I think that learning to be quiet is just a part of stalking, so I won't spend a whole lot of time speaking about silence. All you need to do to learn how to be quiet is to listen to yourself and practice minimizing even your subtlest human sounds. There will be times when this is difficult on dry leaves or crunchy snow. And I don't know how to load a cartridge into the chamber of my gun without a really big metallic noise that is about as unnatural a sound as you'll hear in the forest. You have to load your gun just before you hunt and there isn't a sound in nature apart from a clap of thunder that will cover that noise well. But using naturally occurring sounds to cover yours is a good practice. Most noises can be greatly reduced or eliminated by just slowing your movements.

Whitetails can present sound lure challenges for a hunter. In my experience they do not respond to or generate sounds deep in the woods in the same way that they do when close to human habitats. I don't know why. But I can offer you some audible calls that have worked well for me. While I am at it, I will tell you about sounds used successfully in hunting videos that have never produced good results for me in suburban settings. The following sound lure information is primarily anecdotal. Whenever possible, I will also share why a call does or does not work.

As you may recall from Chapter 5, scent lure selection depended on the time of the year and several conditions. Some attractants such as doe estrus worked best during the rut while others such as food scents were more universal. Some lures had a greater effect on bucks than does. Other scents spooked deer even when the intent was to attract deer. The same is true with sound. Because all of the given conditions are not certain, such as the precise time of the rut and the personality of individual whitetail deer, much of this is an inexact science. But don't let that discourage you. It is part of the fun and the challenge. Success will eventually come your way. Experiment and see what works for your local deer.

Here is the "auditory lineup": bawls, grunts, bleats, wheezes, thrashing, and antler rattles. There are many products that can replicate these deer sounds. Some require you to blow through a resonant tube with a vibrating reed. Other objects produce calls by being rolled in your hands. Here are some of the most popular sound lures. My favorite call is the "bawl"—a cylindrical can with a weighted disk that can slide up and down inside. This lure doesn't freeze up in cold weather and doesn't involve much physical movement. The bawl can be conveniently operated with one hand, which leaves your other hand free to hold your bow or gun. Here's how it works. The sliding disk contains a diaphragm and reed. When the cylinder is tilted, the disk sinks down forcing air through the reed to generate the bawl sound. One end of the can is full of holes to let the sound out, while the opposite end has only one hole that is covered by your finger to create a seal so that the air is forced through the diaphragm instead of escaping while the disk descends. When not in use, the bawl's finger seal hole keeps the unit silent in your pocket or back pack if it rolls around.

The Bawl – right side up     The Bawl bottom with finger vent hole

As with learning a musical instrument, it takes practice to master the variety of noises that can be produced with the bawl. Grasp the cylinder so that you can place a finger over the hole in the bottom (as shown above.) Tilt the cylinder until it makes a bawling sound. Variations of this sound can be achieved by the angle and speed at which it is tilted or shaken. Releasing your finger early from the vent hole will shorten the length of the bawling sound. Tilt the can over naturally, and it will give a long sad bawling sound. This will mimic a doe in heat or a doe asking where everyone is. Releasing your finger from the seal hole during the tilt motion will cause a shorter sound, or a "bleat". This bleat imitates a doe calling her young or addressing other does. Turning over the bawl more aggressively and adding a little shake can generate the sound of an agitated doe— such as when she is in heat or a bit upset. It will certainly catch the attention of deer that are within earshot. This call works well in diverse settings—close to houses and even deep in the forest.

It is also effective for attracting bucks, does and yearlings in any season. Although a yearling is generally not a target for us, its presence in your hunting area will often attract and fool mature deer into entering what appears to be a safe place. Another variable to consider when using any call is the repetition rate at which the bawl is operated. Keep that in the back of your mind for now. I will address that in detail later in this chapter. For now you will need to experiment and practice to produce consistent sounds most suited to the season.

Generally I use the bawl to make a crying, needy doe sound. Two conditions must be met for this call to be most effective: 1) Silence—there should be no wind and the forest should be quiet 2) The time of day—I employ the call within the first 30 minutes of morning light and within the last 30 minutes of light just before dark. At no other time of the day has this call worked for me. If you are looking to get a buck, this will be a successful call during the rut. If you have an antlerless permit (or doe permit) this call can bring does into range as well.

One cold morning when I was bow hunting in my back yard, I was using this "needy doe" call very aggressively and at a high repetition rate because of my impatience. I had to go to work that morning so I had only a short time to spend in the tree. Consequently I was a bit too aggressive with the bawl, and I must have sounded like a doe in distress. A handsome, large coyote responded to the call, clearly expecting to find a hurting doe. He appeared from nowhere like a ghost and was so stealthy. When I finally spotted him, he was within 20 yards of my stand. At that moment he decided that this was a set-up, and he retreated quickly.

One of my favorite adventures when the bawling sound worked well for me occurred on an October hunt during the last few minutes of light. I had been sitting in my tree stand, holding my bow patiently for a little over three hours. I had sneaked into the forest in the afternoon while conditions were quiet with very little wind. The temperature was comfortable, and I was dressed really lightly. On a stump very close to my stand I placed a rag soaked in doe estrus. There was no action at all that day. I didn't see or hear any mammals. The sun had set and I was pretty much resigned to the fact that I would have to climb down soon to walk home in the dark with no deer sighting. With only 10 minutes of light left before full dark, I pulled out my bawl. With one hand on the bow and the other holding the can, I made a couple of calls. Nothing. Not a sound was heard. I let out a couple more bawls, just gazing into the forest and leaning against the tree. Then I heard, "crash, crash, crash" through the brush. A young buck came bounding from the thicket directly in front of me and was furiously stomping within 15 feet of my stand. Clearly he wanted this "bawling doe" to know he was coming. And he was trying to look large. He stopped just a few body lengths in front of me, eyes darting about and the fur on the back of his neck standing up like that of an angry cat. He was hot for this doe and his keen senses had told him right where she was, or so he thought.

As he made his appearance, I slipped the call into my pocket and readied to draw the bow. There was no wind and no sound. As I was debating when to draw the bow, he took a few steps toward the rag soaked in scent. He wandered closer to me, stopping mere feet from the bottom of my stand. Then I drew and placed the pin directly between his shoulder blades. Pointing nearly straight down, I let the arrow fly. It was a great pass through. He ran about 30 yards and lay down dead. Interestingly, I could not see where he fell because it was now full dark. But I recovered him and was completely satisfied with the performance of the call. Notice how well it worked in conjunction with scent.

Another great call to have in your arsenal is the "grunt/bleat" most commonly known as a "grunt tube" or "grunt" for short. Of all the calls sold today, the grunt is the most popular and offers hunters the greatest number of sound variations. It is designed to imitate the vocalizations of a mature buck. Typically, this lure consists of a hollow tube with an enclosed reed that produces a sound when a hunter blows through one end. Most grunts are constructed to make a single pitch. However, fancier models employ a second reed that lets the operator generate a different sound when inhaling, thus providing more options and even "conversation". Some grunt tubes allow the operator to place his finger over the length of the reed to produce assorted pitched grunts. This is helpful when one needs a bleating sound that mimics does or young deer. Beyond the reed is a tube section that on some models is extendable. This component generates a throatier call. Longer tubes project huskier, more mature sounds than shorter tubes. As with the bawl, you will need to experiment and practice to achieve success with the grunt's various tones. Be aware that moisture from your breath can cause the reed to freeze at very low temperatures. Consider keeping it in a warm pocket between uses.

Grunt tube

The best use of the grunt is to attract the dominant buck in the area. If you are after a monster-sized buck, this is a good call to try. So, you might ask, "Why would I use anything else?" Let me answer this way. The purpose of the grunt is to fool a dominate buck into believing a challenger has arrived. Ideally he will get irritated by the threat to his position in the territory, and he will quickly follow the sound to locate and subdue the challenger. When he comes running into range, you can shoot him. Nice set up! The grunt can also bring a buck that is out of range in closer to see who's making all the noise. While it is true that this tactic works to attract bucks, it can also cause unintended consequences. As I said, the call you make will sound much like a mature buck. But if the bucks in the area are not quite as mature as this buck sounds, they may just move away hoping to avoid a confrontation. Or maybe the dominant buck living nearby has become big and old because he does not quickly jump into fights. Instead he sizes up the bucks that challenge him on his own terms. He may approach other bucks to fight only at night, knowing that hunters frequent the land during the day. He may even avoid challenges altogether unless he is breeding.

Now you know the grunt has the potential to scare away some of the bucks within earshot. And what effect does this sound lure have on the females? Did I mention that does rarely come to bucks? If does are not ready to breed, they avoid aggressive bucks all together. Even when in heat they tend to wait for the bucks to find them, and then they will "stand". (As mentioned in an earlier chapter, standing is a hunting term that means the doe will be receptive to a buck and will not run away.) The odds are quite small that you will success-fully attract a doe when grunting like a big buck. She will likely dash in the opposite direction.

My friend Chuck often carries a grunt as he makes his way to his hunting spot. As he stalks, he'll likely make some noise with his feet. If he becomes a bit too noisy he will stop and gives a low, short grunt on the tube. In the event that some deer heard him, they may just dismiss the disturbance as a buck moving about and not a hunter.

Well there you have it. . . just when the grunt seemed to be the perfect sound lure I brought up its disadvantages. But I don't want you to be afraid to use grunt calls. There might be a big bruiser in the area that will respond to the sound. Maybe some bucks will be curious to see who the "new guy" is. I can assure you that the grunt will stir things up. And that is part of the game.

Deer make one other vocalization known as a "wheeze." Man-made hunting wheezes are not used as commonly as bawls and grunt tubes. But I am listing them here for completeness. I don't believe there were any commercial wheezes being manufactured until the last decade. The wheeze is a fascinating call because it is utilized when deer are relatively close. Though not a loud call, it has varied tones and can express a lot of "deer personality". Its appearance and operation are similar to the grunt. The wheeze caught my attention as a short range call best suited to suburban forests. However, of all the calls we have discussed, this one is the most mysterious. I had never heard a deer wheeze until one day I was watering my wife's garden when I heard this strange sound coming from the forest. The sound was repeated with slight variations every few minutes. When I went to investigate, I saw several deer standing together calmly grazing. They looked up at me, snorted and moved away.

It turns out that deer use wheezes to communicate quite a bit, but we don't know what all those sounds mean. One wheezing sound you will likely become very familiar with is "the alarm." Although considered a wheeze it sounds more like a "blow" or a "sneeze"— a strong blast of air that says "RUN FOR IT!" or "GET LOST!" Why do I say that you will probably become very familiar with that sound? Because most everyone will experience being detected by a deer. If he believes he is threatened and cannot hide, he will run. If other deer are in the area, he will "blow" to warn them. This has happened to me countless times in assorted circumstances: during hunts, when moving through the forest at night, and even while I was sleeping in a tent. Yes, one time I was camping out in a tent in my back yard when several deer were apparently upset with me for encroaching on their usual grazing spot. They wheezed over and over and would not let me sleep. It was humorous when they came by at 11:30 p.m. It wasn't as funny when they visited again at 3:00 a.m.

Softer wheezes can be heard indicating other forms of more benign communication. I believe it is a gentle way for deer to encourage other deer to "keep up" or to call the herd together. I once saw a four point buck let out a long slow wheeze for no apparent reason. Then he slowly wandered off as if it never happened. During my research for this book I could not find credible scientific material on deer wheezes. Hunters would benefit from studies about this unique communication. Generally the commercial wheeze call should be used gingerly and with a long period of silence between the calls. I say this because I don't understand what message I am delivering when using this call so I don't want to over deliver such a message. One time I used it and a yearling came to me. Maybe mothers do use the sound to call their young.

A category of far louder, long range, rut-related sound lures includes thrashing and antler rattling. "Thrashing" is the sound that bucks make when they swing their antlers through saplings and brush. This is not the same as rubbing saplings mentioned in chapter 2. Thrashing will attract only mature bucks that really are looking for a fight. "Rattling" occurs when two bucks engage in such a conflict. They will strike each other's antlers with their own. As they butt heads, the antlers will "click" together or rattle against one another. In order to understand rattling and the action that creates it you must observe fighting bucks. I have been privileged to watch a pair of bucks have it out. That was special. If you spend enough time in deer country during the autumn, you will likely see this too. But you don't have to wait. There are hundreds of videos on the web available right now for viewing this kind of encounter. And if you do watch battling bucks, notice the sounds the antlers make and how often they clash. Some fights are intense with a lot of clicking and rattling. Others are more like play and involve less noise. The commotion will draw other bucks much like a brawl draws "human bucks". Guys like to watch a fight, right? Let's face it, when you hear a disturbance that sounds like a fight, you want to investigate it. Well bucks do the same. Does do not come to antler-rattling because they are not interested in watching an altercation.

Experienced outdoorsmen typically will keep the antlers of previous kills for use in future hunts. They click the antlers together or thrash the brush with them in a manor that mimics the sound of a fight. They start slowly with a couple of clicks, and then gradually add more until they achieve a full blown rattle. When they will stop, they hope to have visitors. Or they may have a friend handle the rattling for them while they ready their gun in the likely direction of the approaching audience. Generally deer will approach this fight from downwind, but terrain may dictate otherwise. Remember, once you have made a big commotion, you must minimize your movements or the approaching deer will see you and your antler set waving about, and your efforts will be in vain.

Very likely you don't own a set of antlers right now. Even if you do, you may not want to bring them into the woods for fear of losing or damaging them. You could purchase a pair of antlers designed to be used as calls. They sound quite convincing. However, whether real or synthetic they can take up considerable space in a backpack. Well someone has thought of a compact solution: a "rattle bag". The rattle bag is made of fabric and contains numerous hardwood sticks. The sticks are roughly seven inches in length and have oval or rectangular cross sections. Each bag houses two groups of sticks; one group is slightly heavier than the other group. The different sizes simulate the noise of dissimilar antler tines striking one another. This space-saving rattle bag produces lifelike antler sounds just as well as a full set of real antlers. Roll or rub the bag between your hands to generate the desired sound. Both of your hands will be busy, but I know from personal experience that there will be substantially less physical movement in the use of the rattle bag.

Operating the Rattle Bag

I have tried using the bag many times at early sunup and at sundown. I have never had any real success with it during a hunt. Only once did I have a visitor come to a rattle, and I did not actually see the deer. It happened when I tested out the new call. I believe it was a buck that did not want to show himself. None of my buddies have ever called in a deer with this technique in the suburban environment. Nevertheless, I would not write it off! Clearly this is a very good tactic on large tracts of land. There are numerous professional hunters in hunting videos who demonstrate the rattle bag's effectiveness.

Remember that rattling and thrashing are activities that bucks do during the pre-rut and rut. Do not expect this to work any other time of the hunting season. After all, when the rut is over bucks are interested only in eating and getting ready for the winter. Because bucks have burned a lot of energy courting and mating with the does, they need to get fattened up to survive the harsh winter conditions. They will go back to their favorite haunts instead of fighting each other. Furthermore, bucks shed their antlers shortly after the hunting season. Look around for the shed antlers to acquire free natural sound lures and to learn where the bucks spend their time after the rut.

If you decide to use a sound lure you must consider which type will best attract deer during the conditions of your hunt. Think about how the deer might interpret the call. Even with the best theories, efforts and intentions, your message may not be received as you hoped, but it is still important to learn how to use a call properly and not just play it like a trumpet. Some hunters have success by simply picking up a grunt and blowing. After all, even a blind chicken can find a kernel of corn once in a while. But a good hunter will bag more deer when strategically combining calls, scents and even decoys. Decoys will be discussed in the following chapter.

When employing a sound lure, try not to alert deer to your exact location. Be sure that they cannot see you if they glance in your direction. Avoid using the same call, scent or decoy over and over in the same areas. Frequently re-evaluate and be willing to alter what you are trying to do, especially if you fail to draw any deer.

I am often asked, "So, how frequently should I call?" Well, I'll share my thoughts on that but don't take what I say here are as law. I'm going to tell you what works for me. As I said before, generally I will only use calls during the first thirty minutes of light leading up to sunrise and the last thirty minutes of light after sunset. During that time I call every five minutes and here is my reasoning for this:

We can categorize the deer in a given hunting area as "on their feet and moving" or "lying down stationary". We can also categorize them as "within the range of the call" and "outside the range of the call." Lastly, we can categorize the deer as "those who will come to the call" and "those who will not come to the call". The deer that are not interested in the call and will not come to it are not relevant, so we can disregard those. Likewise, "stationary deer" that are "out of range" are not coming either.

What animals does that leave us? The deer that are "lying down stationary" and "within range of the call." They will come because they are close enough to hear the call, and they will most likely step into view within about five minutes after you have sounded it. Therefore calling more often than five minute intervals is not necessary and may be too aggressive resulting in spooked deer. The "stationary deer in range" are on their way, so limit our call intervals to every 5 minutes and be ready to shoot.

The deer that are "on their feet and moving" but "out of range" may be heading into range and passing through the area where they will hear the call. If we wait more than five minutes between sound lure usages, there is a good chance that deer "moving through the range of the call" would miss the noise and slip back out of range. Therefore, I try to call every five minutes for that category of deer as well. More frequent calling may spook the deer and less frequent calling may result in a missed opportunity. Remember, the calling should be done while the sun is near the horizon. This places limits on how much calling we are going to do, especially if we follow the five-minute interval plan.

This wraps up the information on sound lures. I don't know how quiet Elmer Fudd is when he hunts animated 2-dimensional prey. But if Warner Brothers ever made a cartoon about Elmer chasing deer, I'd be the first in line to see it!

# 8

# Well, How Do I Look?
## (Appearance And Illusion)

There he was, running in, as though he owned the forest. I stood still, in disbelief. Could this really be happening? After all, coyotes are generally not aggressive toward people. They always avoid humans. But, unmistakable in his black and grey coat and fluffy tail, a 43lb. hungry coyote was loping through the February snow heading straight for me. He was closing fast. My heart rate climbed as my eyes locked on this wild dog. I had hoped that it was a local pet that strayed deep into the woods, coming to say hello. No way; it was clearly a coyote, with eyes fixed on me and intentions that were unclear. I would not wait too long to find out what they were. Did he think I was a deer? It all happened in the span of about eight seconds, and then it was over.

One Friday night, my friend Les had just finished telling me about his last cotton tail rabbit hunt in Maine. He calls these hunts "bunny hunts". Les enjoys visiting family in Northern Maine where he hunts deer and rabbit and an occasional moose. During the summer Les fishes up there quite a bit too. Always generous with his kills, he gives the majority of the meat from his hunting and fishing to his relatives and brings home only a little bit for himself and his wife Shirley. Even when he does bring home his meat, he very often shares it with me! He knows that my family really enjoys the wild game.

Les is a grandfather, but I don't know exactly how old he is. He just smiles when I ask. He is in good shape and has a generous heart. I met him at church many years ago, and we bonded right away. He is the hunting uncle that I never had. He is the older man in a young guy's life who is just dying to share his wealth of knowledge of the outdoors, and so it makes him happy to see our enthusiasm when he shows up with goodies. Les encouraged me to deer hunt and taught me how to cut my deer into steaks, roasts and burger. He taught me how to get the bones out of pickerel. And although I was a decent tracker before I met Les, he showed me subtleties that I never thought of. Les even showed me how an old man can go places, such as through swamps and under buck thorn and brambles where this "young guy," as he calls me, would never have bothered to go in search of a buck's hideout. In his retirement, he is clearly superior to me in hiking & hunting. I could go on.

Well, Les had just come home from a weekend of rabbit hunting in Maine. He was telling stories of how the dogs would flush the rabbits out and chase them all over the place. He recounts these tales with all the excitement of a school boy, and I love listening to him. After enjoying yet another long tale of dogs and rabbits and snowshoeing through deep snows, I asked him if he was interested in trying a bit of bunny hunting in the local forests near my home. He had nothing to do the following morning so we decided to head in and see if we could scare up a few cotton tails.

That Saturday morning, we parked my truck and grabbed our compasses, warm hats, gloves and our shotguns. Les handed me a walky talky in case we got separated during the hunt. We loaded our guns with #6 shot and hiked in along an access road for roughly a mile before stepping off into the main part of the woodland. Heading north, we kicked through brush covered in snow, crossed fields of ice that were actually swamps, and generally followed our gut feeling about where the rabbits would be hiding. It certainly was tough without a hunting dog. Nevertheless, I found a significant number of rabbit tracks that gave me confidence that we would see some action that morning. Continuing north, we crossed a stream carefully, trying not to slip into the icy water while balancing our way over the rocks. Once across, we spread out from one another, roughly 50 to 75 yards apart. Our hope was to scare a rabbit that might run to the other guy. We continued this operation for roughly an hour with no rabbit sightings. My shotgun was getting heavy no matter how I carried it. I had my Mossberg 500 pump shotgun with four rounds in it. Les had a Remington autoloader with four rounds as well.

As I trudged slowly through the snow, I kept an eye on Les to my right. We were both wearing blaze orange coats and hats so it was no challenge to see where Les was. He was a tall orange eye catcher against the snow and bare trees. I was starting up a knoll, my legs burning a bit as I dealt with the snow and the slope. Les, roughly 60 yards away, was in the little valley to the right of the rise. I kept glancing his way to be sure of his exact position for safety reasons, and so we did not lose each other. If I were to see a target pop up, my first order of business would be to check where my hunting partner was standing before putting the gun to my shoulder. This is a crucial safety precaution that bears repeating: You must always be sure of a hunting buddy's whereabouts before setting up your shot.

My eye caught movement to my left so I paused and looked. Just behind my left shoulder, about 80 yards away, came a large and healthy-looking coyote. His fur was bristled up on the back of his neck and above his shoulders. He was moving fast and straight toward me with a focused look on his face. I took a half step backwards to put a large oak tree between us so I could determine if he was looking at me or if he had another target in mind. My small movement placed me about 20 feet behind the oak so I could peer around the tree while keeping my body covered. The coyote was running hard and adjusting his course to get the tree out of the way. In disbelief I snapped off the safety and leveled the shotgun in his direction all in the same movement. Wondering how effective my light rabbit ammunition would be against a larger animal, I placed the front bead on his snout and planned to wait until he was within 10 yards before giving him hell. At this point, unbeknownst to me,

Les was wondering why I was standing with my gun shouldered and looking down the barrel. From his view down in the valley, I looked like I was serious about a rabbit.

In seconds, the coyote closed to within about 30 feet, and I am not sure what went through his mind. At that moment, the wild dog had a look in his eye suggesting he realized his mistake. He hit the brakes and tried to stop. But it was too late. I was squeezing the trigger. BLAAAAM!!! (Later I found out that the majority of that round landed in his neck and was the fatal shot.) He turned abruptly and started running behind me. Committed to finishing the encounter as humanely as possible, I pumped the action of the gun and immediately put a second round into his side. He went down in a puff of snow, rolled right back to his feet and continued to run. I fired again, this time at a longer range and at a quickly retreating target. "Dang light ammo. . ." I hissed as I watched snow get kicked up behind the fleeing coyote. The #6 shot was not the best choice for coyote but there was no other ammunition available at that moment.

BLAM, BLAM, BLAM!! As the coyote ran past Les, he gave him three shots in very quick succession from his semiautomatic shotgun. We both watched as the coyote ran hard along a stream and disappeared. We looked at each other silently. Then after reloading our guns, we began tracking the dog in the hope that we got him. After a simple 100 yard track over snow with clear paw prints and an obvious blood trail, we found him lying dead. Les approached him cautiously, scraping the barrel of his gun over the coyote's eye to make sure he was truly dead. And he was. After a high five and a couple of hoots, we rolled the coyote around for some inspection. He was a large male with a good thick winter coat. The fur was very light brown with black highlights. His snout and legs were brown. This wild dog looked a lot like a wolf with his fluffy brown tail and a black tuft on the end. We didn't expect to bring home a coyote on our first rabbit hunt together, but it made our day. We decided to head home and come back for rabbits another time. Who knows, maybe with this big coyote out of the area, we might just see more rabbits!

In the last few chapters we have discussed the first three—the most crucial three—of the four dimensions of camouflage: scent, movement, and sound. Remember, I have put these four dimensions in order of importance. If you control your scent, movement and sound, you will do well. There is a lesser but still significant dimension to camouflage: appearance. Interestingly most folks focus their greatest efforts on appearance over all other forms of camouflage! Many humans are naturally visually oriented. Maybe that is why we frequently err on the side of fooling the deer's eyes. And with the vast array of hunting attire these days, you could get the impression that camouflage clothing is all there is to the art of hiding. This is hardly so as I have demonstrated already. Furthermore, the story of my encounter with the coyote during the rabbit hunt demonstrates that a blaze orange hat and jacket designed to make me stand out did not stop a predator from presumably misidentifying me.

For the benefit of the reader I need to explain that coyotes cannot see the broad range of colors that humans can, but they can perceive a limited set of hues. Any solid color is a poor camouflage "pattern" in the hunting environment because large blocks of uniform hues just do not exist in forests and fields. Thus when we are clad in solid colors, we are not camouflaged. Certainly there are exceptions to this rule. If you are hunting over open fields of snow, a completely white suit may be a good choice.

This brings up the use of blaze orange. Generally outdoorsmen wear blaze orange by law or by choice during hunting season when the hunter density is high. The highest human prevalence typically occurs when hunting with a gun is permitted. Rarely do hunters use blaze orange during archery season. There are three reasons for this. Historically there have been fewer archers than gun hunters resulting in fewer hunter interactions. Secondly, archery requires close range shooting making target identification easy. Third, to get close to deer it is best to be stealthy.

The idea of blaze orange is to make it very easy for a hunter to detect another hunter. This keeps everyone safer. Deer will certainly be able to detect blaze orange but not because of the color. As we have already discussed, deer tend to have better color detection on the violet side of the spectrum than the red side. The orange - if not broken up by patterns in the fabric or by brush between the hunter and the deer - will appear as a large area of grey. It is not an alarming color to the deer, but solid hues are not good camouflage and are more easily detected by the animals. It is a calculated trade off. We want to fool the deer, yet we want to be seen by our fellow hunters.

My son Peter and me wearing a wide variety of camouflage patterns

When camouflaging your appearance, think blend, breakup, and fuzzy. By fuzzy, I mean without sharp contrast; slightly out of focus. Today's hunting clothing market is flooded with materials that have near photographic quality images of branches, bark, leaves and open air patches over every square inch of the clothing. I'll call this form of camouflage "forest imagery". The modern camouflage for hunting is downright picturesque! However I must tell you that such detailed camouflage is really not necessary. But do I own hunting clothing with forest imagery on it? You bet. I like all the camouflage patterns available today, and all my gear has the latest and greatest designs. The colors are very accurate and the shapes are realistic. They look cool, and the competitive manufacturers and retailers know that looking cool sells. They also know that the way to camouflage appearance is to make a pattern that breaks up the human silhouette and helps it to blend with the environment while displaying a low contrast that does not catch the eye. Those are the best elements of disguise—not the fact that the imagery looks like a forest. The manufacturers could produce clothing with random or repeating patterns such as blotches or plaid, which would perform just as well for deer hunting. They could even use colors in those patterns which are not common in the forest such as red, orange, grey and white. However, such designs might not appeal to shoppers. People often ask me what camouflage pattern I like best: Mossy Oak ™, Seclusion 3D™, Realtree™, etc. My answer, "I choose the one on sale." or "I choose whatever is available." If I hunted the exact same environment all the time, I suppose I would choose a pattern that most resembles the area. But I hunt forests and fields, autumn leaf-covered woodlands and late season, snow-covered orchards. I don't have an outer layer for each hunting spot. I just make sure that the fabric will blend, breakup and be fuzzy.

Now let us talk about what it means to "blend" our appearance. Look at the forest around you. There are many different bushes and trees and rocks, each having textures and patterns. There is forest litter all over the ground, and the brushy areas are tangles of branches and leaves. The rocks are assorted shapes and often are coated with moss and lichen. Patterns vary from simple to complex, from light to dark depending on where you are looking. Ideally, those complicated and varying patterns should be mirrored in your outer layer of clothing. The lines and shapes do not have to duplicate your surroundings, but merely to simulate them enough to help you fade into the scenery and not attract animal attention.

The next concept that is subtly different from "blend" is "break up". Just as we want to keep our arms down at our sides when stalking to make us look less human, we want to hide the human shape with our clothing. Hunting disguises have evolved over the centuries. The earliest primitive hunters put lines of paint or soot from the fire pit on their arms, legs, torso and face. In cold regions, they wore the hides and furs of their prey. In the 1900s, they wore tasseled suede or red and black checkered flannel and wool. The goal has always been to disrupt and obscure the appearance of the human form. This best accomplished by avoiding solids and by wearing patterns with which to "break up" our silhouette. If you don't care to wear the modern camouflage and prefer more traditional clothing, be sure that your top layer has a pattern that breaks up the body. Any print with lines, large squares or blotches of varying shades will do. Personally I think the tasseled suede was a great look. Generally, lighter shades work best for brighter environments such as orchards or transition zones, and darker shades work best for deep thick forests with a significant canopy and shady cover. But don't over think this. All modern camouflage effectively obscures the human body shape, and so does the classic wool checkered shirt.

Consider "breaking up" your face as well. As I have said, most animals have an uncanny way of detecting predators' faces—particularly predators' eyes. It is just the way their minds are wired. But we can do several things to hide our faces. Some folks grow beards. This isn't a bad idea. A beard certainly can help obscure the outline of a face while simultaneously providing a bit of insulation in cooler weather. You might find that a beard isn't as good in extremely cold weather since it tends to collect moisture that can freeze into annoying ice crystals. Lines, squiggles and blotches of soot or makeup will usually do a better job of breaking up the face. Whatever you choose to draw on your face do not go overboard. Just put a few fuzzy lines and blotches of black or brown here and there. In this way, your face will not stand out. If you have a very dark complexion, use a light color makeup. Consider white streaks. If you paint your whole face dark, the whites of your eyes will stand out more! Keep about half of your face covered with markings and the rest natural.

Camouflaging the eyes is a bit tricky. All too often deer lock eyes with me. Then the stare down begins. He's trying to decide whether to run or stomp to try to make me move so he can identify me better. Meanwhile I am trying to make up for the error of being detected. I feel as though I cannot move into shooting position while the deer is staring at me. He'll try to fake me out by putting his head down as if to feed, but he's just bluffing. His eyes are on me, and he's hoping I'll dare to move so he can identify what I am. Try to avoid this scenario. It rarely results in getting a shot.

When you detect a deer, it's time to hide your eyes. Squint them until your eyelashes nearly touch. You should still be able to see. The deer will be far less likely to detect your squinted eyes. This will help break up your face as well. Coupled with a little soot makeup, squinted eyes effectively obscure a human face. If you wear glasses, be sure to wear a camouflage cap with a visor. The visor will reduce the glare from the lenses and aid in their concealment. While you are at it, keep your mouth shut. You may want to break into a smile at the sight of a big handsome buck, but your pearly whites will be easily spotted by your prey.

Now that we have covered blend and break-up, we are ready to examine the last aspect of the appearance camouflage trio—fuzzy. Unlike military camouflage patterns which feature distinct contrast, such patterns generally don't exist in nature. Shadows and natural lighting produce soft edges. Therefore clothing with a little bit of pile or fuzz and out-of-focus images provides the best concealment. Nature is not digital in appearance like our military camouflage. One color or pattern must fade into another softly. Apply this principle to every place where you use visual camouflage. When putting makeup on your face, be sure to smudge it a bit. Don't draw sharp lines. If you observe most modern hunting camouflage featuring forest imagery, you will see that the images are slightly out of focus and there is a little pile to the surface. They get it right. Military camouflage patterns stand out in the forest because of their high contrast between the colors. They are not a good choice for hunting.

A little subtopic on appearance is a form of deception that draws attention: a decoy. It is a visual lure that functions much like the scent attractant for fooling prey. Some folks like to use a decoy when hunting deer. Decoys range from full size, lifelike plastic or cardboard deer to something as simple as a white handkerchief hanging from a branch. In many states, using a decoy that resembles a deer is illegal. My home state of Massachusetts prohibits deer decoys. Check your state and local laws. The purpose of a decoy is to draw the attention of the deer away from you and to attract them to a spot that gives you an optimal shot. In states where lifelike animal decoys are illegal, you can still produce a decoy effect. One friend of mine hangs plastic apples from a sapling near his tree stand and sprays the area with apple cider. He has had success doing this. A buck may not be fooled for long, but he will likely come once and check the apples out long enough for you to take a clear shot. The closest thing to decoying I have ever done is laying a white handkerchief over a branch and letting it move with the wind. It is a curious sight that resembles a deer tail, and has caught the eye of both does and bucks. Often they come to investigate it. It has given me success. I have contemplated tying a fishing line to the handkerchief and moving it manually, but I have not yet tried that. Catch the interest and attention of the animal and draw it in, all the while keeping its eyes off of you!

# 9

# Shoot Straight, Will Ya!!
## (Learn How To Shoot Well)

*A* friend of mine has a very successful fruit and vegetable farm. He has many acres of apples, peaches, pears, pumpkins and blueberries just to name a few. It is no wonder that he has deer on the farm all year long. However the most damage occurs when the herd browses on the buds of the fruit trees all winter. Since each bud is supposed to become a fruit the following spring, winter damage is devastating because a single deer can consume as much as eight pounds of fruit tree buds per day. Just think of how much damage a herd of deer could do to an orchard during an entire winter. After the owner listened to my estimation of the size of the deer herd, he decided to invest in eight foot tall deer fencing and electric fencing. This would restrict almost 95 percent of the access to the farmland. However, access to the farm could not be completely closed off, and deer would still be able to get in through a large front entrance, especially at night. So to help with the effort to reduce the size of the herd inside the farm, he organized a deer drive. A deer drive is a hunting technique during which a group of people form a line.

The line marches through the land creating a moving human fence. As a result, the deer are forced into an area where hunters wait in ambush. I was asked to be part of the team of drivers. We kept ourselves roughly 100 feet apart. We walked through the farmland and the small sections of forest within the property, forcing the deer to run in one direction and funnel into the farthest orchard where two hunters were waiting with slug guns.

We began the first drive with seven guys performing the push; the farmer and his son were the shooters. It was January, and the weather was bright and cold. Thankfully the snow was not too deep. Our group of seven was so noisy that we could not be sure we were actually moving this herd of roughly 50 deer right across the farm. Drivers typically have no idea that they are indeed pushing any deer because the animals stay at least 70 yards ahead of the human intruders and always out of sight. On that January afternoon we estimated that they were staying about 100 yards ahead of us.

We marched through the fields of snow keeping our line as uniform as possible. My legs were beginning to burn a bit because we were moving faster than I had expected. Then we moved into a portion of forest where the deer tended to bed down. This was the last piece of forest and final part of the drive before the farthest orchard where our gunners were stationed. Although there were fresh deer tracks in the snow, we could not determine just how fresh. . . seconds? Minutes? An hour? We hoped these tracks were only a few seconds old. At the very least they proved we had initiated a successful drive. The orchard ahead erupted in gunfire. At least 10 shots rang out. We in the line looked at each other and smiled, certain the outcome had been perfect. When the shooting stopped, we walked on expecting to see a lot of dead deer in the orchard. After all, these guys were good with guns. Right?

Suddenly, the forest ahead of us reverberated with the sound of snapping sticks and stomping hooves. Dozens of deer came crashing toward us kicking up snow as they ran. They were moving so fast I knew the safest thing to do was to stand still and let the deer avoid me as they were avoiding the trees in their dead run. It was crazy. One after another they passed between us at blazing speed. Motionless and in awe, I felt the breeze as each raced by, jumping and bounding the whole way. After the majority of the herd had passed, the guys in the line walked on to the orchard. Several deer skirted us on our flank. I stayed put until I knew all the men in the drive had moved ahead. I drew my revolver in the hope of shooting one of the deer flanking us. Watching carefully for the other pushers, I stood waiting for a safe shot. It appeared that a good shot was not going to present itself. Again another dozen deer ran past me at close range but much too fast for me to place a shot well. Then things slowed down a bit. Two deer came to a full stop just ahead of me and stared at me. Clearly they were panicked and tired and unsure where to run to next, so they just froze and stared. I raised my revolver and peered down the sights for a frontal shot at 35 feet. I cocked the hammer. The lead doe broke to my left and shot past me to catch up with the herd. I swung the muzzle with her as she went by, and squeezed a 454 Causull into her side. It was a lethal shot but she ran off after the herd before she went down. There would be time to get her later. I had to meet the boys in the orchard.

Catching up to the others I was surprised to find only three deer lying in the snow. The deer were running harder than we had hoped as they entered the orchard. That, in conjunction with the fact that the guys who were doing the shooting really were not experienced hunters, revealed why just three deer were felled with ten shots — not the ideal shot-to-kill ratio. I found out that these fellas were safe shooters and not necessarily accurate shooters. But that was okay. The deer got the idea that this was not the place to hang out this winter, and I had the privilege of gutting all the deer and selecting one for my freezer. It was a good day indeed. None of the meat went to waste. And I don't think I'll ever forget the feeling of standing in the whitetail stampede.

As a firearms instructor, I have seen various techniques taught to students on how to become a good shot. Besides pistol, I have given basic shotgun and rifle instruction to numerous friends who have not previously used these long guns. Thankfully, they were all bright and eager to learn. They took instruction and correction really well. My teaching experience has made me aware of what techniques are indispensable. My intention is to share those key techniques to help you improve your accuracy when hunting.

There is so much material out there to help hunters improve their shooting skills. There are books that teach how to eliminate the human errors for improved accuracy. There are books that go into incredible detail about reducing all the mechanical causes of inaccuracy within the gun and ammunition. But from what I have read and from the training I have received, I believe that the essentials for the hunter encompass a handful of simple techniques and a reasonable amount of practice. I'm gearing this discussion toward the hunter who wants to be prepared for a successful kill shot at a range of 100 yards or less while using typical, store-bought ammunition and a functional gun.

If you are interested in becoming a competitive shooter with rifle, pistol, shotgun or bow, this chapter's information will help you too. In fact, it will bring you 90% there! Hunting has its own challenges, but the typical rural or suburban hunting environment reasonably simulates the conditions and target distances in non-hunting competitions. Local hunting shots are relatively easier to place than shots fired deep in the wilderness. Rural and suburban hunting occur within short ranges and from directions that have been thought through for safety. Marksmen can have more confidence about taking a shot at over 100 yards in a deep wilderness without people or houses around for many miles. But for our hunting scenarios, we must be careful about shooting safely at short distances.

Toward that end let us start with the three most important NRA Gun Safety Rules. I make sure that my shooting friends and students adhere to these rules at all times to eliminate the risk of accidents. In fact, these NRA safety rules overlap so well that if you inadvertently do not comply correctly with one of them, the others will still keep everybody safe. What I discuss here applies to guns. However, with some common sense these practices can be readily adapted to bow hunting as well. If you have not taken a gun safety course, please do so. Or at the very least, get some help from an experienced shooter. Your selection of a private instructor should be based on his commitment to safety, and the three primary NRA rules can be a litmus test for him. If the shooter you wish to learn from does not hold to these practices you should find another teacher. Choose wisely. Memorize and practice these first three basic rules for firearm safety:

1) Always keep the gun pointed in a safe direction.

 This means that the muzzle of your gun is pointed so that when a shot is fired, it will hit only the desired target. Confirm that no people or pets are nearby that could wander into the line-of-sight between you and the target. At all times be aware of where the muzzle is pointed, even when you are not setting up a shot. You need to determine the safest direction in which to shoot according to your circumstances at the range or in the forest.

2) Always keep your finger off the trigger until you are ready to shoot.

One effective way to accomplish this is by resting your trigger finger flat against the frame of the gun above the trigger and guard. When you are ready to fire, drop your finger down to the trigger—I drop my finger onto the trigger after I have positioned my eyes down the sights. If you rest your finger on the trigger too early and you are ever startled, odds are the gun will fire accidentally because the human nervous system responds to a startle by causing us to make a fist. Let me say it again: Put your finger on the trigger after you are looking down the sights.

3) Always keep the gun unloaded until it is ready to be used.

Remember, the context of this discussion is hunting. Naturally you must have a loaded gun while hunting. However, the gun should remain unloaded until you are truly stalking prey or sitting in a tree stand. Even on the practice range keep your gun unloaded until you are moments away from actually using it. That means you load your gun at the firing line, not while hanging out at the range talking about how you are going hunting next weekend. When you put the gun down on a surface or when you put it in the rack, unload it first. Always unload the gun before handing it to someone else to use. Then if the gun is dropped or is grabbed awkwardly during the transfer, it cannot accidentally discharge and cause injuries or worse. To make it clear that the gun is unloaded, keep the chamber open and the magazine removed, if applicable. And of course, all ammunition should be removed before placing a firearm in storage.

What? That's it? What about the safety lever? What about proper selection of ammo? What about eye protection? If you do the aforementioned three things, you will be doing the minimum necessary to be safe while resolving the biggest safety issues. I can't tell you how many times I've seen experienced folks forgetting to follow these three most important rules. Let me urge you once more to memorize the three NRA safety practices and apply them every time you use your gun. When you have those down pat, move on to these:

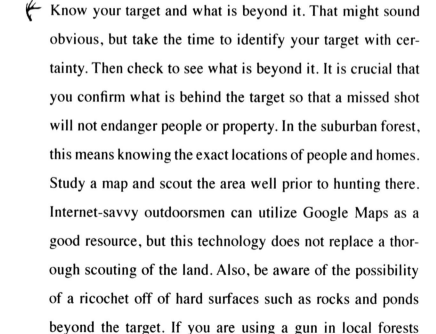 Know your target and what is beyond it. That might sound obvious, but take the time to identify your target with certainty. Then check to see what is beyond it. It is crucial that you confirm what is behind the target so that a missed shot will not endanger people or property. In the suburban forest, this means knowing the exact locations of people and homes. Study a map and scout the area well prior to hunting there. Internet-savvy outdoorsmen can utilize Google Maps as a good resource, but this technology does not replace a thorough scouting of the land. Also, be aware of the possibility of a ricochet off of hard surfaces such as rocks and ponds beyond the target. If you are using a gun in local forests and suburban conditions I recommend the use of short range

ammunition known as slugs. A slug is a large caliber bullet that replaces the shot found in shotgun cartridges. Slugs are low energy rounds that fall to the ground much sooner than typical rifle ammunition. This is because they have roughly half the muzzle velocity and a large mass. Do not underestimate them. The large caliber and mass make them a powerful bullet.

- Know how to use the gun safely. Learn how to correctly operate a particular gun before you handle it. Be sure you know how to determine if it is loaded, how to open and close the action, how to load and unload it, and how to remove the magazine if applicable. Do not rely on the gun's built-in mechanical safety component. It is never a substitute for proper gun handling.

- Be sure the gun is safe to operate. A firearm needs regular maintenance just like any other mechanical device. Clean the gun regularly and store it in a dry, controlled-temperature environment. If you have doubts about a gun's functionality, take it to a knowledgeable gunsmith.

- Use only the correct ammunition for your gun. Strictly follow the requirements in the owner's manual. If you don't have a manual, you can obtain one online. Nearly all manufacturers provide free downloadable manuals for their products. Usually the gun's ammunition type is also stamped on its barrel to help you choose the right rounds when the owner's manual is not at hand. Using the wrong ammunition can be extremely dangerous: it can cause cataclysmic gun failure and serious injury to the operator or those around him.

☞ Wear eye and ear protection as appropriate. Because guns are loud, it is wise to wear hearing protection. But when hunting, you need to hear animals approaching. Therefore, hunters will usually use hearing protection only while practicing. There are products on the market that can protect hearing during gunfire while also providing high fidelity audio and even amplification to the hunter's ears the rest of the time. When selecting ear protection, choose a style that you can wear comfortably for hours. I firmly believe eye protection should always be worn while using a gun at the range or during hunting. Just moving through branches and brush in the woods can injure unshielded eyes.

☞ Never use alcohol or drugs (prescription/non-prescription) before or during shooting. It is common knowledge that alcohol can impair normal mental and physical function, but many medications can have similar effects. It cannot be overstated: You must not use alcohol or drugs while handling or shooting guns.

☞ Store guns so that they are not accessible to unsupervised children and otherwise untrained or unauthorized persons. Use common sense here and check your state's laws regarding the securing of firearms and ammunition in your home. If you believe you need to take measures beyond state requirements to prevent access, do so. There is a wide selection of products on the market for encasing or locking your guns.

- Keep your gun clean. A brand new gun is often greased heavily because the manufacturer cannot know how long it will sit on a shelf and what the humidity and temperature conditions it will have to endure while waiting to be sold. Any gun that has been stored for a long time should be cleaned before use. Moisture, dirt, grease and oil can accumulate in mechanisms and prevent proper operation. Be sure the gun is unloaded before beginning the cleaning process. Ammunition should be kept out of sight so you won't be tempted to load the gun to check its operation.

- There are myriad other precautions to take depending on the shooting activity. Use common sense and do not become complacent so that you may enjoy only good times and fond memories.

Now for the fun part: let's go shoot! Many of you may be experienced with gun or bow. If so, then what you are about to read here will likely be a review. If not, I guarantee your shot will improve if you apply the following principles. Once again I'm going to gear this discussion toward guns. If you are an archer—or intend to become one—you will find that there are many parallels. When I refer to a "cheek weld" on a gun, you can replace that with "anchor point" on a bow. When I say, "increase pressure on the trigger", an archer using finger release should think, "flap". Otherwise, aside from the mechanical differences between guns and bows, the physical techniques and the human experience will be very similar. The key to great shooting is to practice good form and do it often. Here are the steps to becoming a skillful shooter:

Get into one of the shooting positions used for hunting. Be as realistic as possible. Practice all other hunter shooting positions, starting with prone, kneeling, and off hand. Remember to get comfortable. This will improve your accuracy. Archers should consider learning to shoot from above with the bow pointing down at a steep angle. That's right; practice some shots from a tree stand.

Prone, kneeling, off hand (clockwise from the top left)

It can be very enjoyable to adjust your gun sights or scope while resting the gun on a sand bag, on a bench, while you sit on a comfortable chair. This is called "sighting in" the gun: lining up the sights on the gun barrel with the point of impact of the bullet. You should indeed do this to make sure the gun shoots accurately. But sighting in is not shooting practice. You now need to fire that gun from the various realistic hunting positions. It will be much harder to be accurate. Shoot many rounds in all the positions you can handle safely. There will be occasions while hunting when shots might have to be made from less than ideal positions. I remember shooting my open sight slug gun at a deer over 75 yards away. I had the gun resting on my knees while I sat in my tree stand, twenty feet off the ground. To make matters worse, it was a windy day and the tree was moving a bit. Getting steady for that shot while "riding" on a swaying platform was awkward. I got that deer, but I hit it lower than I should have!

Shoot while leaning against a post or tree. Shoot while kneeling or cross legged. Shoot while lying prone, and then shoot prone with your body perpendicular to the line of fire. Do you think the deer won't approach from an unexpected direction?

Whatever position you have chosen, align your eye with the sights or reticle perfectly. The reticle is the targeting image inside a scope – usually cross hairs. Now align the sights or reticle with the target. This is called a "sight picture". This sight picture is difficult to hold perfectly but don't let that concern you. Just relax. Now take a deep breath and let out roughly one third to one half of the air. Hold your remaining breath. This should feel comfortable and natural. Waiting briefly to exhale keeps you steadier and eliminates a lot of gun movement.

Continue adjusting the sight picture of the gun sights and target to be as aligned as possible, increasing pressure on the trigger while holding the gun firmly. There will be a little drift making this alignment imperfect. Continue to increase the pressure on the trigger. Notice, I did not say, "Pull the trigger when the sights pass over the bull's eye." That is not the way to do this! Continue to increase pressure on the trigger while adjusting the sight picture until the gun fires. In the beginning the gun will surprise you. This is good. It will make you very accurate because over time, you will grow accustomed to your gun and become familiar with the amount of pressure necessary to fire it. The movement will become more fluid, and you'll no longer be surprised when the gun actually discharges. Practice this on the range, and then do it when hunting. I can attest that in the heat of the moment, many hunters just jerk the trigger and miss the target. Don't let that happen. Practice self-control.

This whole process should not take more than eight seconds. If you hold your breath longer than eight seconds, fatigue will set in and cause muscle tremors and eye strain. During a hunt if your target becomes obscured, stop, relax, breath, and start all over again. Even if your target remains but you have not shot after eight seconds, breath, relax, and start the process over again.

While you were practicing aligning the front and rear sights with the target, did you notice that it was difficult to focus your eye on all three? Very likely you noticed, and if you didn't, then when you get a little older, you will. Although the eye can have a large depth of focus, especially in bright light conditions, it is usually not possible to focus on the rear sight, front sight and the target at the same time. In fact, when using a scope, you will often find that your eye cannot focus on the reticle and the target at all ranges either. The secret to success here is to focus on your front sight or on the reticle. Allow both the rear sight and your target to go blurry. Believe it or not, this technique will give you the best results. But focusing on the target and allowing the sights to go blurry will result in substantially reduced accuracy. Focusing on just the front sight or reticle may sound easy. However, it will be tougher when aiming at a live target. Try not to get fixated on that big fat deer in front of you. Let it go out of focus for the shot. In fact, it is time to use your tunnel vision that we spoke about back in chapter three. Tunnel in on your front sight or reticle!

As with most sports, "follow through" is important. Continue holding the gun on target for one or two seconds after the shot. I do this with the bow as well. The idea is the same. Hold the gun or bow on target and do not allow your form to change until after the shot is long over. This will stop any movement that is caused by anticipating the shot. It may sound funny because it is not as obviously beneficial as following through with golf or baseball swings, but this plays a role in shooting as well.

One of the most common mistakes I see on the range — and often struggle with myself — is the failure to control breathing. It really is tough to keep from panting when the animal you have been waiting for all year finally appears. Big breaths result in gun barrel movement. Small movements can translate to a change in the impact point of a bullet by as much as a foot at 100 yards. One instructor, teaching me to shoot under adverse conditions, asked me to sprint 100 yards. Then without giving me time to catch my breath or walk down my shaking muscles, he made me shoot several rounds into several targets. The idea was to simulate how I will shoot when nervous or very excited. I got the idea. Unless you are an iceman you will have some excitement to deal with when you are trying to make a kill shot. If you are anything like me, you will be thrilled, jittery and have a slight adrenal response leading up to the shot. It is a challenge to keep the body under control.

What if you can't make it to the practice range today? Here's an idea. How about loading up your gun with some snap caps? Snap caps are "dummy" ammunition designed to absorb the energy from the firing pin. They allow you to practice your trigger pull without harming your gun or risking the dangers of live ammunition. Most guns do not tolerate "dry firing," which means pulling the trigger of an unloaded firearm. Depending on the design of the gun, driving the firing pin into an empty firing chamber can result in component damage. Load your gun's firing chamber with a snap cap for this next exercise. Pretend you are shooting your game animal or paper target. Use proper breathing and trigger control, and focus on the sights in all your positions. Squeeze the trigger and feel the "click" of the firing pin. After the click, follow through for two seconds. This is a great way to help your mind and hands learn when the gun will fire as you squeeze. . . and it can be done at home.

Another element of importance during shooting is the "cheek weld." It refers to how you press your face against the stalk of the gun. The important things to remember here are comfort and consistency. Close your eyes and shoulder the gun. Push your cheek against the stock and open your eyes. Ideally, you should be looking down the sights or into the scope. If you need to move your face more than just a little bit, then the stock has to be adjusted to your body. It is important that whenever you look down the sights, your cheek is comfortable and contacts the stock in the same spot every time. If not, you have added a variable in your shooting and it will show up at the target. Many guys, including me, dabble with adjusting the comb, length of pull and offset of the gun stock. If you don't know much about it, have a professional make the changes. If you are brave, there are many web sites online that can tell you how to adjust your gun to fit your body.

Let us assume that the gun does fit your body well. When you have a variable magnification scope, be aware that the "eye relief", the distance that your eye should reside behind the scope, varies depending on the magnification setting. This can result in your comfortable cheek weld and eye relief being too far back when the magnification is dialed in. Keep that in mind and try to avoid using too much magnification. Higher magnification often leads to problems. A scope with too much magnification can confuse you. You may not be able to see your target in it because it will be like looking down a soda straw. And when you do find the deer, all you will see is fur rather than an identifiable section of its body. Start your target acquisition with your scope dialed out, and increase the magnification only if necessary.

An obstacle to accuracy is the fact that scopes have parallax: the interdependence of the reticle center as it appears on the target and your eye position behind the scope. Yes, go ahead and read that last line again. Scopes are designed to have zero parallax at only one particular range unless they have a parallax adjustment knob. If your scope has high magnification capability, very likely the zero parallax range is at 75 yards or greater. When you are shooting at closer ranges, you might be very surprised at how much the parallax effect will diminish accuracy. Beginners should not use super high magnification scopes, especially in the suburban forests where shooting ranges will be well under 100 yards and even as close as 20 yards. Personally my "bread and butter" slug gun that has taken down the majority of my deer in suburban forests has a 1.5 to 4x magnification. I keep it set to 2x and only change it if absolutely necessary. In fact, for my first seven years of hunting I used open sights. I didn't put a scope on that gun until my dad gave me one for Christmas. That brings up another good point. Don't rush into an equipment upgrade without giving it a lot of thought. People often want the latest scope, the latest adjustment, and the latest gun or bow. Unless something is worn or broken, practice your hunting skills with equipment you already own. A familiar piece of gear will almost always be better than something that is new to you. I can tell you this from personal experience. A new bow caused me a lot of frustration one year because I was not familiar enough with its quirks.

Let us assume some time has passed and you have been practicing. Now that you can knock a mosquito off of a blade of grass at 100 yards, where on the deer's body are you going to place your shot to make the best kill? It is time for deer anatomy 101. The heart should be your target. If you shoot for the heart you will likely hit it and maybe the lungs as a bonus. If you miss the heart, you will hopefully hit the lungs. If you miss both the heart and lungs, there is a slim chance that you could achieve a shot through the liver. But the liver is not the best target because the bleeding will be slower, prolonging a painful death. This is not good because we do not want to extend a deer's suffering. An animal that is not killed quickly tends to travel a long way before it dies. This can make the recovery of the deer very difficult. On one occasion, I shot an arrow right through the spine of a deer. Although it was not an ideal shot, the deer did die quickly and didn't travel at all. I was very fortunate. A question

I often hear is, "Where are the heart and lungs located ON a deer?" The better question is; "Where are the heart and lungs IN a deer."

Often people will refer to the heart and lungs—the ideal kill zone—as "the vital organs" or "vitals" for short. Because a deer is a three-dimensional animal it will present itself to you at various ground level angles: the front, sides and back. Hunters positioned on higher terrain or in tree stands may have the opportunity to shoot downward as well. When I have a chance to shoot from above, I try to let the deer wander off a bit so I can place the shot in its side. I prefer that angle because the deer's side is a bigger target. However, I once put an arrow into a buck shooting straight down between the shoulder blades. It worked out but it may not have been my best option.

There are several things to keep in mind when determining where to place the shot on the deer: The optimum target is hidden deep inside the chest cavity and therefore is not a visible point on the side of the animal. The trick is to visualize the location of the heart and choose a shot that will send the arrow or bullet through that location. The heart is in the lower center of the chest cavity slightly further back from the deer's front limbs. If you have a broadside shot, place it just below the center of the deer's vertical cross section and just behind the shoulder (See the first illustration below). If you have a shot from any other angle, you must imagine the proper entry point in order to make the arrow, slug or bullet pass through the vitals. Practicing your shots on two dimensional deer silhouettes will give you experience only with a single and rare shooting condition. Purchasing a three-dimensional deer target is a must. During practice, set up your three-dimensional deer target and accurately visualize the location of the heart within a deer from various angles. This will prepare you for the real world. For this exercise, the use of a bow and arrow is best because these three-dimensional targets are designed to stop arrows. Walk up to the deer target after each shot and observe where the arrow went. You should be able to see exactly where the arrow passed through the body and if it hit the heart. Did it pass right through the lower center of the chest cavity, just behind the shoulder? If it did, you likely struck the heart. Here are some images to study. The red dot indicates where to place your shot in the most common deer encounters.

Broadside                    Partly Facing
Toward

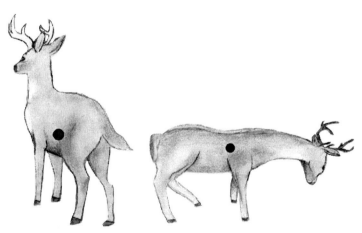

Partly Facing Away      Broadside Slightly Elevated

Facing Toward          Directly Above

Lying Down

Ammunition varies in penetrative performance. The two main hunting ammunition categories are arrows and bullets. Generally an arrow will not penetrate bone well. Thus you should not try to shoot an arrow through the shoulder on the way to the heart, or through the front of the chest where the rib cage has substantial strength. Bullets will penetrate deer bone relatively well, and then expand and do a lot of damage. Keep in mind though that bullets can do a lot of damage to the meat also. Therefore, make a point of sending the bullet through as little of the deer's body as possible before reaching the heart. I cut one deer into steaks damaged by my impatience. I chose not to wait for a better shot angle, and I put a bullet through the deer's shoulder when he was quartered toward me. The bullet reached the heart and lungs but shattered the shoulder bone ruining a lot of meat.

Arrows and bullets are lethal in different ways. The difference is subtle, and often the wounds from both types of ammunition can display similar characteristics on the outside. But inside they are quite dissimilar. Generally bullets are designed to deliver an impulse of energy into the animal to shock the vital organs. This shock wave results in cavitation as the bullet releases its energy into the flesh. The shock causes the organs to fail. Even if the bullet does not actually penetrate these organs, they can be damaged by being proximal to the bullet's path. That is why bullets are designed not to pass through the animal but to expand and stop, thereby delivering the most energy possible into the organs. Obviously organs struck directly by the bullet will bleed as well. A well-placed shot with a bullet can result in a quick and humane death. That is our goal and responsibility.

An arrow on the other hand carries very little energy compared to the bullet because of its very low relative velocity. It is designed to pass through the animal with no cavitation, cutting as many blood vessels as possible to cause lethal hemorrhaging. With an arrow, shot placement is more critical and a pass through is desired so as to increase the rate of blood loss.

I understand that this information sounds a bit unpleasant, but it will help you hunt humanely and recover deer quickly. You owe it to yourself to become a good shot. You work hard all year and have only a short time to hunt. Make it count so you can enjoy the "taste of success" on the grill for months to come. You owe it to the people in the forest to be a safe hunter. And you owe it to the animals you hunt to make good, clean and fast kills. If you think about and practice shot placement, you will do well!

# 10

# You Sit In A Tree?
# You Have Got To Be
# Kidding Me!
## (Tree Stands And Blinds)

*I*t was November and signs indicated that the rut was ending. I sat in an unusually high tree stand roughly 25 feet off of the ground. Typically I sit a bit lower in the tree, about 18 feet off of the ground. But this spot was on the side of a hill, and I really wanted to get up and out of sight of deer that might come down the slope. I had set myself in a section of forest that funneled the deer through a narrow area. My stand faced west, nearly in the canopy of a healthy, red oak. About 30 yards to my right was a pond, and to my left was a large open lawn in which deer would to be too uncomfortable to linger. This slope from the lawn to the pond formed a forested corridor that connected to wider, denser woodland. My hope, supported by track evidence, was that deer would venture through this corridor as they made their way to bed down or feed that morning. The trails clearly indicated a fair amount of deer traffic traversing this area.

Just to be sure, I had a bit of doe scent on a little rag hanging on a branch about 20 yards away.

It was a warm and rainy morning. I confess that I do not really enjoy hunting in the rain, but sometimes that is how it works out. If the rain isn't too heavy, the deer don't appear bothered by it at all. I got into the tree well before light and realized that I was overdressed and hot. The weather report had indicated that this morning would be cooler. Sweating after the walk and the climb into the tree, I unzipped my jacket. My glasses fogged up completely. I sat quietly waiting to be able to see before pulling my bow up from the ground with the rope I had hanging from the stand. The humidity level seemed to be at 100%, and my glasses would not clear. I took them off to wipe them. Through the rain and fog the small red headlight on my baseball cap looked like a device from Star Wars. I thought to myself, "What a great morning to have stayed in bed." But I believed the deer would be moving today, so it was best to take advantage of the waning days of bow season. I pulled at the rope, feeling the weight of the bow lifting off the ground somewhere in the dark below. I eased it up slowly, carefully keeping the sites from striking the tree. I could not see the ground or the bow. The light on my head just lit the fog below. Holding the rope away from the tree, I kept pulling. My mind played tricks on me, making me feel so much higher above the ground than I actually was. Finally the bow was in my hands. Settling it into my lap, I turned off the light. Checking my cell phone

I noted that there would be another twenty minutes until first light. Everything was still. Only the rain moved the few leaves left on the trees. I became motionless and even thoughtless. Everything settled down inside me. The sound of the rain filled my ears, and the heavy drops dripping from the branches made heavy "plop" sounds as the water struck the forest floor. The confidence in my safety harness that secured me to the tree, the darkness, and the warm rain began to lull me to sleep. [I do not recommend intentionally falling asleep in a tree stand. However, it can happen so be sure to prepare for the possibility.] Although I did close my eyes because there was nothing to see, I forced myself to remain awake and listening. The sound of the rain and dripping was so steady and loud that another person could have easily scaled the tree without my hearing him. Time passed and the night ended. The weather had not changed, but I was now able to see. I scanned the area all around me. No animals. I settled my gaze in the direction of a shooting lane just up the hill from the lawn and began to zone out. The rain was hypnotic. I snapped to attention several times as the dripping from the trees repeatedly tricked my mind into thinking I was hearing hooves on the forest floor. Over and over my attention was drawn to yet another hoof-like sound. Each was a false alarm and I grew weary. An hour passed and although the rain continued, the fog cleared completely. I once again cast my gaze on the shooting lane to my left. Little did I know a large bodied buck with a great set of antlers was ambling down the funnel straight toward my tree. He approached silently and came within 15 yards directly in front of me before passing to my right. (Yes, I determined all this after the incident.) I actually did not become aware of him until I heard the splash of his hooves as he walked across the brook leading into the pond. I turned my head to see him stepping up from the brook on the far side. At this point he was over 50 yards away. I grunted immediately hoping to call him back. He completely ignored my calls and moved out of sight. Staring at where I last saw him I was quite upset with myself for being so unaware. Grunting one more time, I stared after him, and then scanned around to see who might have followed him that morning. Nothing. Argh! I made an agreement with myself that I would force my eyes to scan at all times, even in the rain, as if that were really possible.

Moments later, I noticed the buck circling around the perimeter of the lawn and coming back. My heart raced. I stood up slowly and prepared the bow. Evidently he had been attracted by the scent lure and wanted to double check the source. What a nice buck! He was an 8-pointer with a healthy, large body. He stood still 40 yards to my left, standing in the shooting lane I had been staring at lazily just moments before. Unfortunately he was facing me head on. He was very casual for a buck looking for a doe. I drew on him, just waiting for him to take another step forward and turn to show me his side. Still exposing only his front to me, I stood at full draw, mouth dry and the rest of me soaked in this now teeming rain. But

Mr. Buck refused to come closer. He stared for another minute in the direction of the funnel and the area below my stand. Then he grunted. Seeing no response, he gave up on the scent source. He reversed direction and walked away leaving me no shot, just very tired arms. After mulling over the whole event for the next two hours I just chalked it up to experience. The lesson learned that day was: Try to stay alert even on a rainy morning, or stay in bed instead. I left the tree and went home.

Lauren and I in a two person stand

A typical "hang on" tree stand for one occupant

As I was preparing to write this chapter, I realized that I had to step back for a moment and note that for the beginning hunter, some of my anecdotal outdoorsman experiences may sound a bit odd. I know this because many people have asked me to teach them how to hunt. Their inquiry generally follows a pattern. I tell them about the time spent in the forest scouting, setting up a blind or tree stand, carrying out the actual hunt, and on-site processing of a slain deer. I explain that I often exceed 40 hours afield between kills. Then I get a queer look. They ask in astonishment, "You spend all that time in the woods? Do you get bored?" Then they crinkle their noses as if preparing for a bad smell to accompany my explanation. Their eyes glaze over as I explain the nuances of the hunt. Most are polite and feign a bit more interest. That is when I smile and ask what they do with their free time.

The vast majority of those who are interested in learning to hunt don't take the next step, which is to enroll in a hunter safety course. Just this week a guy who has watched me cut many deer into steaks, and with whom I often go to the shooting range said, "Hey, can you teach me to hunt? Well, you don't really hunt, right? I mean, you sit in a tree." I thought to myself "Here we go; the non-hunter will now teach me how to hunt correctly." But because I've known this fellow for so long and we are close enough to rib each other a bit, I just laughed and replied, "Come scout with me Saturday."

Aside from the thrill of bringing home a deer, nothing compares to the excitement of just watching the forest from the higher vantage point of a tree. You will see a lot of wild things. I don't know many people who have sat quietly in a forest for any length of time, not to mention a full day. Ironically, in today's fast-paced, high tech environment, clearing the mind for thinking, reflecting, watching and waiting is acceptable only if such open-ended mental relaxation takes up no more than a minute or two of one's busy schedule. I understand that thinking. At the beginning of every season my mind races the first few times I go into the woods. Until I can slow down enough to appreciate the pace of the woods, I feel impatient. But then it begins to happen. I relax. I believe the greatest way to spend time thinking, reflecting and watching is to sit in a tree. Many gun-friendly folks who don't actually participate in hunting have said kind things to me such as "Well, even if you don't get one, I know you; I bet you are just happy to be in the forest and have some quiet time." And what they say is true. Well, it is almost completely true... extreme weather conditions can certainly disturb my peaceful state-of-mind. Regardless, I usually respond with something such as, "Yah, if it was all about the kill, I would have hung up the sport long ago." Anticipation of a thrilling encounter with a game animal that may culminate in a kill shot keeps me in the woods. Yes, I enjoy the environment. Yes, I enjoy seeing the wildlife and spending quiet time with God and His creation. Yes, I even enjoy just pondering my own selfish thoughts, concerns and goals. All that is really special, but the ultimate goal is to bring home a deer. And when everything comes together—the thrill of the encounter, the buildup of tension prior to the moment of truth, the shot, the follow up and recovery — a successful hunt is absolutely indescribable.

I spend the majority of my hunting time in a tree stand because the weapon I use most is the bow. The bow is a short range weapon, and quietly occupying a tree stand is the easiest way to get close enough to deer for a successful shot. In the following pages I'll cover the basics of using this elevated platform such as how to locate a tree that can support a stand. I'll also introduce the alternative of a ground blind when there are no trees sturdy enough for a stand.

First, there is the matter of safety. Using a tree stand requires an understanding of how to attach the stand apparatus to the tree correctly, how to climb safely, and how to occupy the stand safely.

This should be taken to heart. Many more people die or sustain very serious injuries falling from trees while hunting than they do from improper firearm handling. Most of the time, injuries are caused by carelessness. Manufacturers of tree stands have come a long way in making their products safe, and they provide wonderful documentation and even training DVDs that you can learn from. Don't throw these instructions away. Study them. I cannot teach you in these few pages the proper operation of every stand model on the market. I do insist that you use a full body harness and that you buy new stands when they get rusty and old. And never build your own tree stand platform out of lumber unless you are using tree house quality construction techniques and are willing to inspect the structure annually. After you visit a friend in the hospital with a broken spine, these extra safeguards won't seem like a bother. Enough said.

There are a variety of reasons for hunting from a tree stand. The primary reason is that the elevated vantage point provides a greater view of the area than can be found on the ground. The height can also reduce the number of obstructions that would block a shot. If those were the only reasons, I would be sold on the idea. But there is more. Tree stands tend to present little to no disturbance to an area. Most deer that have not been exposed to hunters will not be looking up in the trees for predators. "Uneducated" deer that are not aware of elevated hunter techniques are concentrating their vision between a horizontal plane and the ground level. And because they make great use of their olfactory sense, they are often putting their nose to the ground. Being above the deer's head gives us a tremendous advantage. It typically allows closer proximity to deer than can be achieved with ground hunting methods. There have been times when I have had deer directly beneath me. Nevertheless, a tree stand hunter must not become too complacent on his perch. Excess movement and unnatural sounds will catch a deer's attention. He won't forget the day he saw a man in a tree! Then the "educated" deer will make a point of avoiding the area, or at the very least, start looking into the trees when he comes by. I remember the day I watched a big-bodied, gnarly-antlered buck emerge from a thick swamp and walk along its edge. He peered into the clearing where I was hunting and looked around, eyes elevated, as though he was bird watching. Yes, he spotted me. That was the end of that encounter. Another time, I observed four does entering my hunting area. The lead doe put her nose to the trail on which I had walked. She picked up the scent of my new boots on the ground. Then she immediately picked her head up and looked up into my tree and directly into my eyes. I hadn't moved. Clearly she knew the tree stand was there and she checked immediately to see if I was in it. She turned right around and took her lady friends and yearling back the way she came. Obviously you need to be careful not to give yourself away, and sometimes you are spotted anyway. But in approximately nine out of ten tree stand deer sightings, the animals do not know they are being watched.

You read in chapter 5 that I firmly believe hunter scent control is a critical part of success. One additional benefit of the tree stand is that any scent you might still be exuding will waft over the heads of the deer in the area and will mix with the air further away from the stand. That distance will help your previous scent control efforts be even more effective. Your scent profile will become nearly non-existent. As a final precaution I use a cover scent on my boots, the lowest point of my body on the tree stand. This is a good idea anyway because our boots make a lot of contact with the ground when we move through the forest.

Recall our discussion on shooting safety from the previous chapter. We must always be sure of our target and what is beyond it. When hunting from an elevated location, the forest floor serves as a back stop just beyond the target. Naturally the angle of incidence will result in a gun harmlessly shooting the ground if a miss occurs. And bow hunters know that a well-aimed arrow will typically pass through the vitals and exit the deer's body. Unlike bullets, arrows rarely lodge in deer flesh. Therefore when shooting from a tree stand you can rest assured that the arrow or bullet will be buried in the earth beyond the target.

It's time to explain the basics of tree stand use during hunting. Suppose you have done some late summer and early autumn scouting through the forest and found some deer paths, droppings and other sign. You have also studied the lay of the land and can see where deer go to feed or to seek cover. Now you know where to spend your time during the hunt. Can you find a tree in the area that is healthy, straight, strong, and roughly a foot in diameter? If so, you have located a suitable candidate for a tree stand.

Always avoid these unsuitable candidates: a tree that is not perfectly healthy, a tree that has many dead branches, is losing its bark, or has a significant number of woodpecker holes. Also avoid a tree that is too large to wrap your arms around because it will be very difficult to get straps into place. Reject thinner trees that will sway with a lot of weight up top. If you sit in a thin tree, you might look a lot like a giant corn dog or taffy apple in the middle of the woods — unnatural shapes that will probably scare away deer.

Take your comfort into account as well. If you have several good tree options in the area, consider which one would keep the sun on your back instead of in your face. Will you get a favorable view of your shooting lanes? I'm right handed, so tree stand shots that are more to the right of center can be a bit awkward for me.

Of the many tree stand designs on the market, I prefer ladder stands because of their stability. They are silent, unlike climbing stands that ratchet their way up and down the tree every time you get in or out. The ladder model is much faster and safer to install than the "hang on" stands that need to be clamped onto the tree. Ladder stands are a bit more awkward to carry to and from hunting spots, but once they are in place their utility is superior to other models. This is a personal choice but I strongly suggest making your first stand a ladder stand.

Once you have followed the manufacturer's instructions for securely attaching your stand, you are now ready to leave the ground and begin ascending the tree trunk. Be sure that you are wearing a climbing harness. Leave your bow or unloaded gun tied to a rope at the base of the tree. When you are settled into the stand sitting safely and have secured your full body harness to the tree, you can pull the bow or gun up to you. Climbing with a bow or gun strapped to your back is very tempting and time saving. But if you fall with these things attached to you, the injuries will likely be more serious. Furthermore, when you use a climbing harness, the strapped-on weapon will interfere with your climbing. I tried this awkward and dangerous method early in my hunting career. Thankfully, I'm older and wiser now.

Although I have put an illustration of a two-person ladder stand in this chapter, typically tree stands are designed for one occupant. Single person stands are substantially lighter and as a result easier to haul into the forest and connect to the tree. For this reason, my two-person stand is located on my own property. I have used it to teach my children how to hunt. In any case, after attaching a stand to a tree according to the manufacturer's instructions, climb into it and be sure it is secure. Do not bounce in it to test it since that creates an unnecessary strain on the straps and joints. Instead, while seated and strapped in, lean your weight from side to side and front to back. There should be no movement and no squeaking sounds. If there are, get out of the stand, loosen the attachment mechanism and secure the stand again.

Generally I leave my daypack at the bottom of the tree. Among other things, my day pack contains water and snacks. By keeping the pack out of reach I concentrate on hunting and am not easily distracted by the goodies. If I take a break to eat, I will get down from the tree and stand on the ground. Many hunters prefer to attach a hook onto the tree at about head level where they hang their daypack for easy access. Others who are very serious about scent control and not contaminating an area will keep a urine bottle in their day pack so that they can relieve themselves while in the tree. Personally I am happy to descend the tree, walk a reasonable distance away and dig a shallow hole with the heel of my boot. After leaving my refuse, I will bury it much like a cat. This provides sufficient scent elimination in my experience. Whatever you choose to do, be sure to scan the forest from your perch before moving about to eat, descend or just stand up and stretch. Be sure your quarry is not going to catch your movements and hurt your chances for success.

Some terrain, such as an orchard or scrub brush area, simply won't contain suitable trees for your elevated platform. In that case, consider using a "blind". As its name suggests, a blind is a simple ground-based structure usually made of area debris that should keep you hidden while allowing a clear view of your surroundings. The greatest challenge of any blind set up is keeping it from getting in the way of your shot. And honestly, I have never been satisfied with my ability to see or shoot from the best of ground blind set ups. There will be some limitations associated with ground blinds. But there is at least one advantage: Because you are already on the ground you will never have a serious fall out of a blind. However a blind does raise your risk of being shot by another hunter. I recommend that you place an orange hat or vest on the top of the blind to make other hunters aware of your presence. If another hunter is considering a shot in your direction, he won't know you are in the line of fire without such an indicator.

De-scenting and using a cover scent are more critical when on the ground in a blind. You do not have the advantage of your scent wafting above the deer as it does when you are in a tree stand. Also, the majority of deer will approach the area of interest with the wind in their faces, especially if you are using an attractant scent. There-fore, plan the blind and its shooting openings with the prevailing wind in mind.

Do you remember when I said that deer will know we have "rearranged the furniture in their living room?" Well, this is true here. The deer will notice that you built a blind. The blind will hide you, but it won't be invisible to the deer. Ideally you should build your blind a few weeks before you intend to use it so the animals will become accustomed to it. But real life is rarely ideal. So if you are hunting mid-season and you come across a promising piece of forest, go ahead and build a blind. Give it a try and sit in it for the day. Not every deer will take issue with the new lump of debris you added to the area. But try to be subtle. Build your blind in the visual dead spots and far enough from the paths.

So, what shall we use for the blind? We have a lot of options. Start by finding a comfortable place to sit where you can stay still for a long time. A stump or a log is often the best choice. Just don't use a rock. Rocks are very uncomfortable due to their hardness and their tendency to drain the heat out of your rear end. You can also eliminate the guess work and bring a chair. Next, plan the directions in which you want to shoot. Now form a lean-to. Make sure your hole through the blind is unobstructed by debris and large enough for your gun plus a clear view of the target area. Your shooting openings should be wide enough for reasonable target acquisition but not so wide that you will be essentially "in the open." Some folks build a blind tall enough to cover only their bodies, and leave their heads exposed above the semi-doughnut-shaped brush pile. This is very effective too and offers a broader range of shooting options. However, your face and eyes will need to be camouflaged, especially at close ranges. Again, make sure that other hunters know you are in the blind by using blaze orange or the equivalent above your location.

The forest is usually loaded with ground debris and downed branches for constructing your blind. But if there isn't enough material or if you want to be more mobile, there are various styles of pre-fabricated ground blinds that can be purchased. Most models look like a glorified camping tent. Some use camouflage fabrics and come with an integrated seat. Other systems have mirrored surfaces that can be set at a certain angle to reflect the ground cover to the prey. For successful invisibility on the ground keep in mind the four dimensions of camouflage discussed in previous chapters.

One time I was in Northern Maine near the Canadian Border hunting black bear. The teepee style ground blind I sat in was well-constructed and supported by a six inch diameter tree. The teepee was missing one quarter of the back wall making it very easy to walk into from the rear. A twelve inch hole in the front provided a view and a sturdy log served as a gun rest just below the opening. It was sweet. My rifle rested in the hole and was balanced, although I never let the gun out of my hand. Down wind and a "chip shot" distance away was a spot that bears were known to visit. I sat in that blind from lunch time to dark for five days. I was comfortable in a plastic chair and partially covered from the rain. And it did rain one day. I even came in the morning once just to be sure I wasn't missing an early visit. Had the bears not been perfectly nocturnal, I might have had a shot. But I did not get any opportunities. There was plenty of wildlife to see that week but no bears. I can't blame the blind!

# 11

# I Have Ants In My Pants
## (Hunting On Foot)

*D*ecember mornings near the Canadian border can be quite cold. That autumn was milder than usual. But it was cold enough that a lot of game animals were moving about. The thermometer read 20 degrees at the cabin. The air was dry even with the water boiling on the top of the wood stove. When you plan a trip like this you always hope for optimal weather. Warm weather late in the season is never good. Chilly weather is best. I was happy to see that the day was to be cool and overcast with a chance of light snow in the afternoon. Perfect. Sometimes, when it is too warm, animals with heavy winter coats tend to lay down to stay cool. I have been out hunting on days when deer just didn't want to move because the temps were over 50 degrees. When they stay still, the hunter must move around to locate the stationary quarry, get within shooting range and finally make the shot. The additional activity makes it harder to avoid detection, but it is an exciting challenge. This chapter is dedicated to those times when you don't want to sit still or shouldn't because of the weather conditions.

That cold and clear Friday morning my friend Nick and I, with Bill our guide, were after elk! It was my first elk hunt and I was excited to get into the woods. Maybe it was too obvious. As the guys dilly dallied over their cups of coffee at the breakfast table, I was already dressed and outside working the bolt of my. 30-06 Sturm Ruger rifle and making sure the scope was clear. I had my ammunition in my pocket and my daypack was ready. Dressed too warmly to stay indoors any longer, I stood on a knoll close to the cabin and glassed the landscape hoping to see any critters who were enjoying the morning as much as I was.

Finally, all the sundry things were in order. The truck was loaded and we headed an hour north to a spot Bill had planned for our hunt. We enthusiastically talked forest management, game management and even a bit of politics and religion. I guess hunters can talk politics and religion and still be buddies after. Eventually we arrived in a beautiful piece of forest dotted with meadows. The trees were a mix of hardwoods and a few conifers. The boulders and outcroppings of rock reminding me of the forests back home in Massachusetts. Some sections had really old growth clear cuts put in to create meadows. And the animal sign was everywhere. What a place to hunt! I was so excited I thought I could see a game animal behind every rock.

Stopping briefly at another cabin tucked into this pristine forest, we "eliminated" the coffee we had that morning and got down to business. With my gloved left hand holding my rifle and my bare right hand holding a hand warmer in my coat pocket, we made our way down a logging road looking for bull elk. Being very confident that there were a variety of game animals in the area, I scanned and listened continually. After an hour we saw a group of four whitetail deer. They bolted away before we could study them. It was much like the old adage, "If you are not hunting deer, you will see a bunch of them." Another hour passed and we saw a second group of whitetails way off across a clearing. They didn't seem too disturbed by us, although they watched us continually. The cold and the time passing took a toll on me. Being on high alert for this long began to wear me out. It had been about four hours since we started hunting in earnest, and I must have been straining instead of using my full field vision and unfiltered hearing. Sometimes when I am too eager, I throw technique out the window and get sloppy. When that happens, I remind myself to relax and enjoy the day. An over eager hunt or shot will not be your best performance. And after a few false sightings of game, I started to feel a bit foolish.

But then, I spotted an elk. The moment I stopped to give it a second look Bill was already staring at it. Nick lifted his binoculars and we began whispering. "Is that an elk or a log?" "Might be an elk." "I think I see antler." "It's lying down, see it?" "I think that's a log Joe." "Maybe." "Let me see those 'nocks." "Ya, it's a log." "No! It just moved. I can make out some antler." It had been agreed upon beforehand that Nick wanted a very large bull. I was after any bull. So I was given the nod to take this modest animal. I got down on one knee and steadied the rifle. I dialed up the scope to 9x. It had been set to its minimum magnification of 3x. I had plenty of time. This bull was lying down and unaware of our presence.

Through the scope I saw the bull elk. . . a 10-pointer with a healthy young body. He was lying on his right side with his foreleg over his heart. This elk was resting roughly 140 yards away on a gradual hillside that rose above a meadow between us. His bed was about 60 yards from the meadow in relatively open forest. I stood opposite him on the far side of the meadow, snapped off the safety and gently rested my finger on the trigger. The brush only slightly obscured a view of the vital area on the elk. But his elbow certainly obscured the heart more. Bill stood behind me and crouched down with his head just over my left shoulder. He whispered "Take him if you like the shot." I took a breath and let out half. Repositioning my finger on the trigger, I asked "Should I take a head shot? I don't see the vitals well." "I don't recommend it." Bill replied. I took my finger off the trigger and sheepishly whispered. "I don't like the shot. Can I get closer? That elbow and brush is throwing me off." My bullet would very likely have penetrated the brush without too much trouble but everything inside me said, "DON'T TAKE THIS SHOT."

Bill tugged on my jacket and we began moving left, slowly walking 90 degrees from the line of fire. We spotted a large oak that split into three trunks, each greater than one foot in diameter. This tree was about 40 yards in front of the elk. We planned to try to close the distance by stalking in behind that tree. Keeping my eyes on the bull the whole time, I began to feel the burn in my legs and the adrenaline in my lungs as we continued to stalk to the left. Eventually I aligned that tree with the bull elk's head. I could see only a portion of his antlers beyond one side of the tree. Now it was clear what to do; Bill didn't have to say a word. My job was to move silently toward that tree and focus on the elk's antler and body the whole way. If he moved, it would be time to consider a shot. If not, I would close in until the shot was easier. The wind was favorable, blowing gently from right to left keeping any scent away from the prey. I moved along quietly in a full stalk, with the safety off and my finger on the frame. The rifle was tucked tightly to my chest as I slowly closed the distance. After about five minutes I was thirty yards from the tree, and the elk's clearly visible lower body looked larger than life. The head was still hidden behind the tree. Bill motioned to me "NOW!" without saying a word. This would be an easy 70 yard shot. I took one step to the right and knelt down, placed my finger on the trigger, aimed and fired almost in one movement. BOOM! I had put the crosshairs just to the right of his elbow hoping to bypass it and have the bullet enter the heart. But that didn't happen. The bullet crashed right into the elbow joint. Not knowing for sure if it continued into the heart. I immediately worked the action and fired again as the beast stood up on his hooves with his left forearm raised. BOOM! The second bullet passed through both lungs. Not wanting to risk a long track, I sprinted ahead and to the left closing the distance to 15 yards and broadside as the elk began to try to run on three limbs. As I pressed the trigger for the third shot, he fell to the ground. Before he hit the ground, a third bullet passed through the vitals—again. That third shot was not necessary but it was a result of wanting to be humane and to be sure he did not run far. Bill was jogging up behind me yelling: "He's down. You got him. Nice work. Stop shooting. I'm happy he didn't go over the next rise or we would have a tough haul to get him out. That was YOUR ELK. It was meant to be. I can't believe how close you got to him. That was meant to be!" The elk was cleanly killed, and Bill was a very excited guide. I asked Bill if he would join me in a prayer of thanksgiving. We both bowed our heads as I knelt beside that big body. I will never forget it!

Although the majority of my kills are from tree stands, I have enjoyed much success from the ground with methods such as still hunting, deer drives, and deer pushing. As indicated by the elk story above, hunting on foot is exciting when you know the bucks are hiding in the brushy swamps, or the wind and rain have all the deer bedded down. Maybe you're an energetic person who would rather go get your quarry instead of sitting in a tree waiting for deer to come to you. Like many things we learn for the first time, hunting methods may sound odd and seem hard to understand until you get out and try them for yourself. The good news is that the "hands on" approach is fun and speeds up the learning process. For instance, Chapter 6 introduced the basics of stalking. I explained the "half stalk" which is done with the body erect and the "full stalk" with the curled posture. You will get plenty of practice in both of these stealth techniques when still hunting.

To still hunt, one must really take the word "still" to heart. By this I mean that the hunter should be spending his time standing still and looking, listening and even smelling his environment. And only after establishing with great surety that there are no deer to be seen, should he take a stalking step. The step should be done as slowly as humanly possible. If you cover more than 100 yards per hour, you are likely moving too fast for still hunting. For this reason, the majority of my stalking is the "half stalk" because I am most comfortable when my body is erect. Hunched over in a full stalk for a long period of time is exhausting. Spend a lot of time just standing, watching and listening. Look very carefully. Then move. If you make a sound, just freeze and wait. After all, deer make some noise too. The still hunter just has to make sure his noises are small and rare, much like that of a deer's. I recommend making a bleat sound after breaking a stick or causing other undesired noise. This may fool anything within ear shot into thinking that you are just another deer.

Still hunting is effective in forest environments where there is a bit of cover. But I think it is most effective, as well as most difficult, in thick cover. So pick a spot with dense growth that is difficult to penetrate. As with any other hunt, you should scout the area first. It is best to have scouted the area at the end of the previous hunting season. In this way, if you spook deer and alter their patterns it won't matter. This is a good practice for any type of scouting. If you find deer sign, plan on still hunting that piece of land next season. The thick, barely penetrable stuff is where the wisest and therefore biggest deer will spend their time. And frankly this may be the only way to get some of the big bruisers who know better than to enter the open shooting lanes.

Always note wind direction when starting any type of hunting. Although you should be using all the scent control that we spoke about earlier in Chapter 5, keep the wind direction anywhere except directly on your back. Use a cover scent as well. Next, spend a full minute taking in the entire view. Now squat down slowly and look again. I do this mostly just to keep my blood flowing, but it also gives you new angles to see through brush. If you don't see any deer, take another step. If you think you spotted one, close in for the shot. If this is painfully slow, you are probably doing it right!

You will be detected by deer on occasion. They may snort and bolt. But this type of hunting confuses deer. They are usually unaccustomed to human movement like this, and upon detecting you they might actually come closer to investigate. Even if they bolt away, they won't travel far—usually only about 50 yards—before stopping and looking back. Be ready with the shot. I will conclude these stalking tips by being completely candid with you: still hunting is not for everyone because it requires so much stamina and patience. But it's certainly worth a try. Put in some hours to see how well you handle its rigors.

In Chapter 9, I told a story of a deer drive at a local fruit and vegetable farm. With an eight foot fence on the left side of our route through the forest and a large open field to our right, this drive was quite effective. I included the story to introduce a group hunting tactic known as a deer drive. This is a great technique to use when the deer are completely spooked and pressured in the late season. At that time they don't want to do anything but bed down and hide. The drive will get them moving. Deer driving can be used in a variety of woodland habitats, and it is especially suited to land that abuts residential neighborhoods where shooting would occur too close to houses or roads. The deer can be driven out and toward areas more conducive to shooting.

It takes some advance planning to gather and coordinate a group of friends for a deer drive. Some will be drivers; others will be shooters. There is no required number of people for a drive—I was one of seven drivers in my Chapter 9 account, and there were just two shooters. The group size should be sufficient to cover the selected territory. A drive begins by forming a line of hunters spaced between 30 to 50 yards apart, depending on visibility. They must be sure they can easily see one another and be able to keep the line relatively straight. These drivers should start walking simultaneously through a piece of land where deer are expected to be. The man in the center of the line should have a compass to ensure they all remain on course. The drive line should make noise and tromp steadily through the target area. It should be noted that the drivers rarely see any deer because the animals tend to stay far away from loud, rowdy humans. But the folks up ahead in the shooting positions will likely see numerous trotting deer or maybe even a stampede. For this reason, drivers may not bother to have guns with them. Their job is to drive the deer in one direction—not shoot.

Be aware that on occasion a deer will get disoriented or decide to run through the drive line. If you are an armed driver, you will be tempted to take a shot at this deer. I strongly recommend that you just let it go. In fact, if a lot of them try to break through the line, just freeze and watch them run by. If you stand still, you won't be trampled because they are very good at avoiding trees even at full speed–and you will be just another tree in their eyes. Typically when a passing rogue deer briefly presents his broadside for a good shot, your fellow driver will be directly behind your target. So not only would you be trying to hit a high-speed sprinter, you would also be endangering a buddy in the line of fire. Be wise. Let the shooters up ahead do their job and have the meat waiting for you. Don't get greedy.

The shooters on the far end of a drive have a challenging job that begins with three safety elements. First, they must know the exact direction of travel of all the drivers. Next, they must ensure the shooting lanes are parallel to each other and facing the same direction, which means all the shooters must be on the same side of the drivers' path. Ideally, the shooting should occur at a 90 degree angle to the travel direction of the drivers. Lastly, the shooters must make their exact location clear to the drivers. This ensures the line will stop a safe distance from the shooting lanes at the end of the drive. Then after all the gun fire is over (if any) the drivers give loud hoots and wait until the shooters call them in. Needless to say, wear blaze orange for this operation. A deer drive is very productive, and the meat obtained is divided among all the participants. You may not get a lot of steaks but you can be pretty confident you will not get skunked!

It bears repeating here that driving deer should be a late season activity. For one reason, deer become harder to find as the season matures. Some are killed off. All are tired from the end of the rut, and they are pretty aware that hunters are in the woods. However, the most important reason is etiquette toward tree stand hunters, still hunters and other small scale outdoorsmen. Deer become quite spooked and their natural patterns are disturbed by deer drives. They most likely won't go back to their calm, natural feeding and relaxed travel patterns until long after the hunting season ends as a result of drives. Therefore early season drives significantly disadvantage tree stand hunters and others who have scouted, studied, and planned how to get their deer. These folks are not going to be happy to find that the animals have all gone into hiding or have become completely noc-turnal as a result of the drive. Personally, I have known the feeling. Once while sitting in a tree stand I heard several deer running through the forest. Next I saw a fox scoot right past my tree without slowing down. Then about a minute later I heard the tromping and hooting as a line of orange clowns come through. One smiled and tipped his hat to me. The circus had come to town. It is legitimate and legal to drive deer through areas utilized by lone hunters, and I have done it myself. But this was opening day of shotgun season! I was completely at a loss of what to say or think. The season was about two hours old, and the only hope I had for the rest of the day was that just maybe a deer broke through the line and wasn't going to go into hiding. Unfortunately this brute force method of hunting not only nullifies more subtle methods for that day, but in some cases for weeks. Late season drives allow equitable hunting for all.

In all fairness I have to tell another story of how I scored a nice doe when I was not involved in a drive. And if not for the drivers, I might not have had a chance. While in my tree stand one afternoon I heard a deer crashing through the forest. A doe appeared at 40 yards. She stopped, looked over her shoulder and then kicked her rear legs in the air like an irate donkey. As she started to bolt up the hill before me, I took her down with my shotgun. I wasn't even out of the tree to check on her when the drive moved through. One of the fellows said, "You're welcome. Enjoy!" smiled at me and walked right past the spot where I shot her. I returned the smile and yelled "Thank you! You pushed her right to me!" Because I was not involved in the drive, I felt no obligation to share the meat and they didn't expect any. It is understood that tree stand hunters and deer drivers are not very compatible. So when a nice thing like this happens, all parties involved should extend grace. In fact, when the bad things happen we should extend all the more grace.

One last "on your feet" type of hunting I would like to talk about is the push. Pushing deer is similar to the drive. However it requires far more scouting, experience and preparation. It is done with only one person "pushing" the deer and another doing the shooting. If you know an area where deer tend to hang out, take a walk into it. Hearing you coming, they will move out of that area. The question is, did they go right, left, straight away or did they circle? Determine this with your observation skills. Then walk to where they relocated. Where did they go from there? Find out. Do this as many times as it is practical. Now you have gained valuable information about deer habits while practicing pushing (without the shooting part.) For example: If you have determined that deer hang out in a small blow down, walk into that area and push them out. After you ascertain that they head left toward a stand of pines, follow them there. Then, if you observe that they take a right across a narrow brook to get behind the houses, move into that destination also.

Preparation for deer pushing is important, and it can be done at any time of the year. Unpressured deer are inclined to walk away — rather than flee — from what they perceive as "harmless humans." So a spring or summer off-season stroll through deer habitats can yield a lot of information that could make your subsequent hunting season more productive. Plus you will be experimenting and practicing with the optimum pace and distance for pushing deer on your terms. Have you ever been to an orchard at a local farm and spotted deer? When you do see quarry in that orchard, walk toward them casually and naturally. Don't move too quickly; act like a typical human. You might see that they head northwest into a stand of hardwood trees. It isn't guaranteed that they will do that every time, but odds are they will. File that information in your memory. Seize opportunities like this to practice the right amount of "push" toward a favorable area, rather than sending deer into a dead run.

When it is time to hunt, place your shooter friend in an area somewhere down the chain of egress. In the small blow down and brook scenario mentioned earlier, a good position would be near that narrow water crossing. After he has quietly settled in, begin walking, or "pushing" the deer from that small blow down. Then take a left and walk toward the thick pines. Continue pushing toward the water crossing. If all goes well, you will hear "BOOM!" before you finish your walk.

There are no guarantees with any method of hunting. Pushing is notoriously frustrating for me. There have been times when I was sure I had the deer figured out only to find out they were not even in town on the day of my push. On another hunting trip, my buddy accidentally spooked the deer while settling in for his shot, and they headed toward me when I was not ready. Then they suddenly changed direction altogether! When this happens, just smile and note the escape route that they used for next time. When you are in the woods, you should always be gathering knowledge and experience. Failure isn't bad if you learn something from it.

# Oh Great! Now what?
## (Deer Recovery)

*I* had a busy day planned. After dropping off my kids at school, I needed to do some office work and a bit of house work. My wife worked only until noontime this Tuesday. So my plan was to have lunch with her, take a shower, get into my tree stand by about 2:00pm and sit until sundown. I had an "ace in the hole"—a pristine hunting spot that was loaded with deer! It was a piece of woodland surrounded by homes, with no access except by walking through a landowner's yard. As far as I could tell, I was the only hunter in there. This forest was a 12-acre deer paradise. I was fortunate enough to see a fisher cat here as well the week before. My tree stand was on the south side of an old growth, pine grove located near a wetland with heavy cover on all sides. The small forest clearly had little if any human traffic. Maybe it was the high tick population or the dense mosquito population that kept folks out. No matter, the deer population called me in despite the bugs. The temperature would be in the low 40s that day, which makes the mosquitoes less active.

However, I would be flicking ticks off of my hunting pants by the time I reached my tree.

I arrived at my friend's house. Every deer season he allowed me to park my truck in his driveway and slip through his back yard into the forest. I grabbed my bow and day pack and quickly made my way across his property. After stepping into the woods, I paused as I always do to give thanks and to soak up the moment. It was a time to relax and shift into the hunting mindset. I knelt down and peered into the quiet autumn forest for a few minutes. My senses began to fill up with the sights, sounds and smells. I caught the movement of a coyote scooting away. He had been watching me and decided I was bad news. I smiled to myself. He humbled me. I was not sure how long he had been watching but I'm glad I slowed down so I could see him briefly. I stood up and began the tough stalk to my stand. The stand was only about 200 yards from the houses but I had to pass through thick brush and a dense sapling forest with absolutely no human trails. There were animal trails but they were not heading where I wanted to go. Plus I was bigger than the critters that had made the trails. I did my best not to crash through all the saplings and underbrush. As I moved along, I looked up at the canopy. This beautiful forest had an unusual abundance of maple trees. The red leaves were stunning today.

Arriving at my tree, I climbed into my ladder stand and locked in my safety harness. I settled in and nocked an arrow in my bow. It was sunny and cool. The wind was blowing a bit harder than I preferred. I felt the breeze and the tree swayed a bit. The maple and beech leaves floated down from the canopy with every gust. Time passed. The wind came up and settled down. Birds visited me. A red tail hawk flew into the clearing, came in low about two feet off of the leaf and pine needle floor and swooped up to a branch. He stood motionless for five minutes. Then he locked eyes with me and immediately flew out of sight. I saw nothing more for another hour. The sun made its way through its autumnal arc in the Southern sky. Not a sound was heard except the gusty wind.

My gaze rested on fiery red maple leaves on the edge of the pine grove. Then I saw a flick of a tail. My eyes widened. Did I imagine it? I tunneled in and saw a deer leg lift and lower in the thicket just slightly to my left at 45 yards. I began to put weight on my feet to stand up slowly, my heart rate increasing, my bow hand adjusting its grip for a shot. Within a minute I was on my feet. The doe slowly made her way to the edge of the pine grove and lifted her nose to investigate the faint scent of doe pee I had placed on a branch ten yards from my stand. As if from nowhere, another deer appeared to her left, then another and yet another! A yearling sniffed the ground on her right. So amazing are these animals at hiding. What a rush to see them all. After a moment of glee I had to refocus. I angled my body hoping that they would walk to the right and present a broad side shot to me. Minutes passed. They grazed a bit on barberry and something in the pine needles that I could not see. Jackpot! They began to move toward my right presenting a good angle. More time passed and I began to think about when to draw the bow. The wind was still a bit gusty. And now with the deer this close, I was thankful for the breeze. The moving branches gave me confidence that I could draw the bow without being noticed. And then the moment came. The largest doe was just about where I could get a clear shot at her heart. I drew. Resting the dot just behind her forelimb slightly below center, I placed my finger on the release trigger. Then a second doe stepped beside her on the far side. I hesitated. Arrows don't usually stop in deer and I didn't want to wound the second deer with an arrow that had passed through one deer already. I waited at full draw, lowering the bow to rest on my thigh. In this position, I could hold a full draw for minutes. With my bow arm straight out, muscle tremors would begin in about twenty seconds and making a clean shot would be impossible shortly after. The doe in front took another step forward. All clear. I raised the bow and placed the dot in her side at 25 yards. Release! The arrow disappeared into her side and vanished into the earth behind her. She was off like a flash, bolting straight forward, then turning hard to the left to run back into the cover she had come from. I watched her disappear from sight, crashing through the brush. I could see the saplings sway as she ran through them. I kept saying to myself. "Go down. Go down!" I wanted a clean and fast death and a short track. After a minute my breathing began to return to normal.

I sat down, as the rest of the herd moved out of the clearing, not sure what had happened. Then I entered into "deer recovery mode," a critical series of steps the hunter must carry out after the shot. The difference between finding a shot deer and finding nothing can be determined by just a little extra care in process and observation. The process I am about to share with you is a set of guidelines that I go through every time I shoot an animal. Because they are guidelines, I don't follow every one of them to the letter each time. Use your head and make sure that they make sense for your situation. But if you have any doubts or this is your first harvesting experience, you can use the steps here exactly as described to aid in your recovery of the animal.

Because the doe ran out of sight, I made conservative assumptions that she was still alive and that the shot was not perfect. It could be that she ran only 50 yards and died. But if she had run only 50 yards and lay down to rest and lick her wounds, it would be better not to walk up on her. So I looked at my watch and made sure not to leave the stand for 30 minutes. Again, some conditions may change how long you wait, if at all. But in this case with the deer out of sight, the thing to do was to wait. If the deer was only wounded, she could lie down and bleed to death resulting in a short track. If I walked up on her too early, she could run a long way before dying, making her hard to find and possibly damaging the meat.

During this time of sitting in the stand, review what you saw after the shot. Where exactly was the deer standing when you took the shot? In what direction did it run? What was the last spot where you saw the deer before it disappeared from view? Mark your compass and make a mental note of that location. You will walk to that point later. You have now gathered all the information you can observe from the tree stand. After thirty minutes have passed you should get out of the stand and walk to where the deer was shot. Find the arrow as well as where the deer was standing. Do not destroy the tracks with your own feet. Carefully examine what you see. Look at the characteristics of each track identifying where the deer was standing when it was hit. If you run into many deer hoof-prints later, maybe something about this one will help you determine which deer track to follow.

Examine the arrow. Did the broad head deploy properly? If it is a fixed blade, did it hold together? If the blades are heavily damaged, you probably hit thick bone and not just ribs. Is the shaft covered in blood? An arrow shaft that is covered only in fur may indicate a miss. An arrow covered in fat or greasy stuff may not have hit lung or heart. An arrow covered in green or brown goo might have hit the stomach or bowel. An arrow that is covered in blood is a good sign because it has likely passed through the heart or lungs.

Take a moment and pull out the role of orange marking tape you keep in your back pack. If coming back later to collect the orange tape is too much of a chore for you, toilet paper can be used. It degrades quickly in the next rain, eliminating the need to go back and get it. Pull off a six inch length and tie it to a branch above the spot where the deer was standing. If there is no branch, just drop the strip of tape on the forest floor.

I am going to assume that you are tracking all by yourself at this point. If you are tracking with a friend or multiple friends, you must pick a point man. The point man is the lead tracker and the other trackers must stay at least 10 yards behind him. The reason for this is to avoid destroying tracks, blood evidence and overturned forest litter. And having a group of guys simultaneously following one animal does not work well if they are all bunched together. The role of secondary trackers is to observe and follow the prints and wounded deer evidence, and confirm that the primary tracker is on the right path.

Find the next track. Very likely the deer jumped. Look for blood both on the ground and on any vegetation along the travel route. Place marking tape on every location where blood is found. If blood is not found, place a piece of marking tape over every track within ten yards of the previous one. Continue on the trail. If you lose the track and cannot find blood, go to the location where you last saw the deer running away and pick up the track there. If you still don't find a track or blood, take a few steps in the direction you assume the deer traveled. Be careful not to destroy track or blood evidence with your own boots—a very common mistake.

In addition to trailing your wounded deer visually, keep your ears engaged too. Listen carefully. Do not make a lot of noise. If at any time during the tracking process you hear the deer moving up ahead, stop! Make a note of exactly where you are. Then go home and come back in a couple of hours. Audible deer movement thirty minutes after taking your shot means your animal is wounded and not yet dead. To follow it now will result in pushing the deer and reducing your chance of recovering it. Being patient will ensure the best outcome.

Continue along the blood trail. If you travel more than ten yards without seeing a track or blood, you may have lost the track. Go back to your last mark and look again. If you still cannot find the track, make expanding concentric circles. Expanding concentric circles is a simple system to pick up a track of a deer that has jumped a long distance without leaving evidence over that span or has made a radical change in direction. Remember, deer can go straight, turn or double back and turn. The double back and turn is the toughest to follow. But by using expanding concentric circles you can efficiently subdivide the observation area to relocate the continued path of the deer. From the last piece of track evidence, step five paces in any direction and walk slowly in a circle keeping the last track mark as the center point. Did you detect anything? If not, count off another five paces and walk a circumference that maintains a ten-pace radius from the last track mark. You must be very observant. Be alert to any disturbance in the forest floor or plant life. Remember, deer do not fly. They may bound over a long distance but they must touch the ground. If a deer has done something to make you lose the track evidence, this expanding concentric circle tactic will cut the deer's trail or bring you to where it lies. Even drastic changes in the deer's travel will have to be cut by the circle you are making.

There is another simple trick I employ when following a track that seems to have vanished. Often, when unsure where an animal has gone, I will walk the easier path. Like us, deer will sometimes chose a path based on how easy it is to traverse. This is especially true when they are calm. It can be less likely when the deer is escaping. Either way, look at the terrain and ask yourself where you would have gone. Furthermore, much like humans, most deer are right side dominant. In other words they are right-handed or right-hoofed and tend to turn to the right when faced with an obstacle. If you can't find the track as you approach a large tree or bolder, turn right and see if you can pick up the trail. If you still cannot relocate it, then try the left-hand direction. While the aforementioned tracking approaches are not perfect they do save time and have aided me when I have lost the trail.

Now let me tell you how this Tuesday afternoon hunt ended. I took a deep breath after all the deer left the area. My heart rate settled down and I texted my wife to let her know I took a shot. After recording in my mind the exact location in which the deer had been standing, the direction that it ran and the last place I saw it, I added a mental picture of the tree right next to the spot where the deer disappeared from view. I also recorded in my mind where I last heard the animal crashing through the forest. After thirty minutes and a brief prayer, I quietly stepped down from the tree stand and walked to the location where the deer had been standing for the shot. Finding the arrow, I noticed that the blood looked very red and coated most of the arrow. The broad head blades were in good shape and had deployed properly. Looking at the ground, I found the depression where the deer pushed off to begin its run. There was no blood on the ground. So I marked the location with a piece of orange tape and started along the path I saw the deer take. To my disappointment and surprise, there was no blood trail. As the deer exited the pine grove, it entered into an area where the forest floor was covered with red and yellow maple leaves. The blood red leaves that made my heart sing earlier in the day now made my heart sink. Every leaf looked like it had blood on it. I bent very close to the ground to determine what was foliage color and what was real blood, yet I found no blood. Fortunately I was able to follow the turned up leaves and torn up earth. I rounded to where the deer had disappeared from sight. More red leaves littered the ground, but still there was no blood trail. At this point, I was like a blood hound, putting my face right to the ground, convinced that I was missing the blood trail due to the camouflaging effect of the red leaves. How could there be no drops of blood with that shot? I continued to track for about 20 yards before it was clear that the doe had slowed to a trot, and her hoof prints blended with the many other deer on this run. My heart began to sink further. Did I hit it well? I stopped and scanned the landscape. Then I saw a huge pool of blood and the dead doe facing me just off the trail. It was one of my easiest recoveries and the only one that gave me such a poor blood trail. I happily dragged the deer out of the woods just before dark.

Even if you shoot your deer and you see exactly where it drops and dies, I recommend that you go through all of the recovery steps listed anyway. It is good practice. If the deer does not move at all for five minutes, you can get out of the tree right away and begin the recovery. But try to fight the urge to run directly to the downed deer. You will deprive yourself of the experience you can gain by tracking the deer the whole way from where it was shot to where it dropped.

One final thought about approaching downed quarry. When closing in on the animal, assume that it is playing dead. This is especially important if you shoot a predator or a very large animal. A predator may attack you, and a large animal may get up and run over you. For this reason, I approach a downed animal from any direction except straight to the face. I have my bow or gun ready, and I scratch the eye of the animal with the arrow or muzzle. No animal that is faking can stand having its eye scratched.

Well congratulations, you have your deer! It is time to give thanks and celebrate. In the next chapter, you will learn about deer processing. But for now, revel in the success of the hunt. Oh, and if you are like me and prefer blaze orange marking tape over toilet paper, be sure to go back and collect the markers. The impact that the kill has had on the environment, including the scent of the blood left on the forest floor will be erased over both time and rain. The area will return to normal. But that orange tape should be collected to eliminate human litter and to be sure not to confuse other hunters or land surveyors.

# Gut Deer?
## (Removing The Organs
## That Most Of Us Don't Want To Eat)

*I*t was a warm day for late October. It was 60 degrees, or a bit more, but it felt like 80! There I was, sitting on the top of my ladder stand swatting mosquitoes. I couldn't stand it. It didn't help that I got a call on my cell phone from a friend Dave telling me he had arrowed a doe at roughly 7:00am just a quarter of a mile away from my position. Unfortunately he had not found it. Dave had been tracking the shot deer for two hours and he had lost the trail. He called in another buddy to help him out. That guy brought his dog to try to pick up the scent. From what I surmised, this dog was not a trained tracker. Dave was in a rush. You see, after two hours Dave had to abandon the track so he could head to the airport for a business trip. He needed to be in California and would not be back until the following week. Needless to say, he was unhappy. His friend with the dog had to go to work too, and the whole deer recovery effort was called off. I offered him my help but he said "Thanks anyway but between the dog and we two trackers, it just must have been a bad shot." So I offered him my condolences and hung up the phone. For the next hour I swatted at mosquitoes that were trying to crawl into my ears while the temperature steadily rose, and I kept picturing a dead deer about a quarter mile away from my stand. Frustrated by my unproductive morning amidst the swarm of blood-thirsty bugs, I decided to go and look for that deer.

Before starting the search I needed to go home and change into jeans and a t-shirt. Having put on warm hunting clothes earlier that morning I was now sweating from the short walk out of the woods. By most standards it was a beautiful day with no wind, and I was hoping for the best as I returned to seek Dave's stand. I traveled light carrying only a compass, my hunting license, pocket knife and a bit of confidence. I was glad to have found the tree stand easily because I had never visited Dave's latest stand location. But he had given me enough information so that I walked right in and found it. After a quick glance around I paused to pray for help and guidance as I do before any track. If I didn't find this deer, I would at least have put some more tracking time under my belt. I always try to capitalize on opportunities to track a shot deer. You will be fortunate if you can track such a deer once a year, and you will learn a lot. Also, calling off the dead quarry's recovery should be done only after extensive effort and the determination that further tracking will not likely result in finding the deer. We owe it to the deer and to ourselves to follow these principles.

Dave did a fine job marking the deer's location for the shot with a piece of orange marking tape. Upon examining the ground and vegetation I was able to pick up on the track nicely. My excitement began to build. For me, the start of the track is exhilarating with a touch of apprehension. I often think to myself as I bend down to examine a track, "Somewhere down this series of tracks there has to be a deer." Every ten yards or so the trail was marked with tape tied to the blueberry bushes that adorned this piece of woods. And yes, after roughly thirty yards, a significant blood trail was accompanying the places where the hooves kicked up leaves and left partial hoof prints. These subtle impressions were formed when the pressure from the hoof was released on the hard ground. There had been very little rain so the soil was not yielding much. The gait of the deer appeared to indicate that the animal was not in too much distress. The further the deer traveled the less blood it was dropping. That was not what I was hoping to see. I continued along slowly, all the while trying to ignore the obvious orange tape markers in the event that they were not correct. As the blood trail became very sparse, I slowed down further and was careful not to damage any of the weak track evidence along the way. After about 150 yards, the marker tape ended along with the tracks and the blood trail. I stood still and looked intently. The only tracks I could find were a few boot prints zigzagging about. I barely detected a dog track. Had I not been told that a dog was brought in, I would have missed its paw prints. I remained motionless for the longest time trying to determine where the deer would have gone. I reasoned that the deer could have taken a hard left toward a hole in the thicket about a stone's throw away. Or maybe knowing that she was heading toward the road, she took a hard right. Could she have doubled backwards without my detecting that her tracks were going in reverse? After standing, thinking and looking in that small area for about ten minutes I decided to walk 40 yards ahead to get away from all the human tracks that may have damaged the trail. I then checked out the possible escape routes toward which this doe may have turned. After a thorough search and finding no tracks or blood, I speculated that she made a radical change in direction at this juncture. But there was no evidence to support my thinking. I understood Dave's frustration. Up until the last portion of the track, the deer was moving to the left in a gentle curve that went up a hill, and then she made a gradual shift to the right as if she were wandering more than fleeing. The doe appeared to be casually walking by then.

Going back to where the trail disappeared, I checked out the hole into the thicket off to the left. Nothing convinced me that she went that way. Although there were some prints, they didn't look like hers and there was no blood that I could detect. So I went right and wandered about looking for any evidence of deer. Nothing there either. I began to realize that I was starting to track up the area with my boots and zigzag just as the other guys did hours before. For some reason I didn't make expanding concentric circles as I usually do when I lose the track. Instead I began to think that the deer might not have been mortally wounded. I prayed, "Lord, I am at the limit of my ability. If this deer is dead I need You to guide me to it." Then I added, "But I think I'm going to just walk out to the road and head home. It was fun." The road was 75 yards ahead of the doe's last detectable track. I walked straight toward the road scanning the ground, my hope fading. I could see the hard top clearly now. As I approached the road, there she was, 15 feet from the pavement's edge. I neared her perfectly still body slowly. She lay on her side in the shade of a maple tree. The doe appeared to have laid down to rest and died. What a great reminder to never give up hope! A car drove past adding a bit of irony to my long stint in the woods and the wonderful end to my morning. I thanked God for another great boost to my faith and the short distance I would have to drag the deer before loading it onto my truck. I called Dave to share the good news, and to let him know that his doe would be packaged up for him when he got home. It was time for me to get messy. I tagged the deer and gutted it on the spot. Wiping my hands and knife on my pants, I thought selfishly, "I wonder if I will get a steak out of this deal. . .?"

Cutting open your deer is a powerful reminder of the fact that you have taken a life. You will feel the warmth of the body and the lifelessness of its limbs, followed by the sobering awareness that something has to die so we can eat. If your heart feels a bit heavy, that is normal and appropriate. Deep down you may realize that in God's Creation, animals and man were never supposed to die (Genesis 2:17). If you felt ambivalent toward death I would be concerned that you did not understand the value of life and the gravity of taking even an animal's life although it is lesser in value than your own (Luke 12:24). Even so, God has made it clear that it is good to use the animals we kill and to honor Him with careful stewardship of His creatures. It was God who made the first clothing out of animal hides, and who can accuse God of doing an injustice? So have a clear conscience and use what you have killed as fully as you can. In order to preserve the meat you must remove undesired body parts and waste material shortly after the hunt—a process known as field dressing or "gutting." Frankly gutting a deer is messy, and it is the part of the hunt that most hunters don't get too excited about. But you can do it, and you will be fine. Let us pretend for the moment that your time has come.

Congratulations! You have taken your first deer! And you have tracked it down and found it. Hopefully, you have given everyone in your tracking crew a high five. Or if nobody is with you, you have performed the Tarantella complete with tambourines and singing. Now it is time to get to work. Hopefully you are in a location where predators are not going to challenge you for your downed deer. Unload and secure your bow or gun and set it aside. Pull out your license and detach the appropriate antlered or antlerless deer tag. Fill out the date and fold it tightly, stuffing it deep into the deer's ear canal. You will know if you have put it in far enough if you need to use a pocket knife later in order to dig it out. Now take the elastic band out of your back pack and wrap it around the deer's ear so it is closed tightly. You should secure this tag as if keeping the deer is dependent on how well you secure the tag—because it is. I believe that in all states, moving a deer with no tag attached to its body is illegal. If you are found in possession of a deer by a warden or environmental police officer and you cannot produce a deer tag on the animal's body, the deer will most likely be confiscated. A fine is certainly possible. So be sure the tag does not get lost. Next, you may want to scratch your initials into the bottom of one of the deer hooves. If you have to leave the deer and retrieve it later, you do not want some unscrupulous individual to claim it as his own. In the event that someone does, you have evidence of your possession.

Having finished what the law requires, you can now begin the field dressing or gutting of the deer. Field dressing sounds much nicer than gutting, but it is somewhat of a misnomer as you will see. The process involves opening the deer's abdomen in order to remove the visceral organs. The first step is to decide where to do the deed. Should you field dress the animal right where it died or do it someplace else? Should you leave a pile of guts near your tree stand or further away? Can you field dress the deer in a less conspicuous place where people and their dogs are unlikely to come across the entrails? Will it disturb nearby homeowners if a big "coyote feeding festival" happens tonight in this spot? These are important considerations. Most of the time, the answer is to do the field dressing right where you are. One third of the deer's weight will be lost by taking out the gut, making the effort of dragging the body much easier. So unless it has grown too dark and you forgot your flashlight, or you lost a broad head full of razor blades somewhere in the deer's body, you should start to remove the gut. Pull out your nicely-sharpened knife and a pair of rubber gloves. Always wear latex or rubber gloves while field dressing the deer, especially if you have a cut on your hand that might come in contact with deer blood. Usually deer are healthy animals, but they can carry bacteria and even viruses that are detrimental to human beings. Err on the side of caution and protect yourself.

I am somewhat particular about using the right tool for every job. Thus I prefer to utilize a different specialty knife for each of the deer-processing steps. I have one for field dressing, another for caping (removing the hide), and various other knives for boning out and steaking the meat. Can you do it all with one knife? Yes. But with all the options out there, the right knife will make the job go quickly and easily. I recommend locking-blade, or better yet, fixed-blade knives for all your hunting needs. Fixed blade knives are invariably sturdier and easier to deploy with one hand than folding knives. For a typical adult deer, I use a field dressing blade that is three to four inches long with a drop point. A drop point knife has a spine that drops down to the tip as opposed to having an upward curve. A knife with a gut hook is nice but not necessary. Furthermore, the dimension from the cutting edge to the spine of the knife should be less than one inch. You do not need a lot of torque strength or deep cutting length for field dressing deer. This is much like surgery, so a short, fine and sharp knife is best.

If you do not have an experienced hunting friend to guide you, there are countless videos available demonstrating how to field dress deer. The best way to learn how is to watch someone do the job and then try it yourself. If you are squeamish about blood and guts, this will get you over it. You can get over it. . . I did.

The goal of gutting is to eliminate the organs that are not going to be eaten and to do so without disturbing or rupturing them, which could compromise remaining edible portions. Some people use every part of the deer, and I applaud that. Regardless of whether you wish to keep everything or not, the gut must be separated from the meat to cool the meat down as quickly as possible after the death of the animal. This will yield the best culinary results. The majority of the guts are in a flesh "bag" often referred to as the "gut bag." When done properly, the gut bag separates from the body with very little mess and remains intact, which keeps gastrointestinal and urinary goodies, and the majority of the blood away from the meat. This is important! If you allow these materials to make contact with the meat for any length of time it will be tainted. The results can be anything from a bad taste to meat spoilage. But don't panic. In the event that unhealthy fluids and feces get on the meat, it can be salvaged with no bad effects if the material is removed immediately and the meat is rinsed thoroughly with water or snow. Mistakes will happen on occasion, and it is very common for a beginner to cut the gut bag accidentally resulting in a stinky mess. Just remember to wash out the cavity when you are done.

Now let's go through the gutting steps. With your gloves on and your knife in hand, roll the animal onto its back. It will be wobbly and not inclined to stay in position. Straddle the deer so you are facing its lower half—toward the tail end. Place your feet on either side of the rib cage to keep it stable enough for the first cut. With one hand, feel for the bottom of the sternum where the bottom ribs come together. Pinch up the hide here and insert the knife with the blade facing upward. Now you should have a hole in the hide just below the sternum. Place your index finger on the spine of the blade with the tip of your finger just barely covering the point of the blade. Having your finger under the blade keeps the tip of the knife from cutting more than one layer of tissue at a time. With the sharp edge facing up, slide your blade and finger into the hole you created. Cut the hide open in a straight line from the belly to the anus. If it is a buck, remove the genitals.

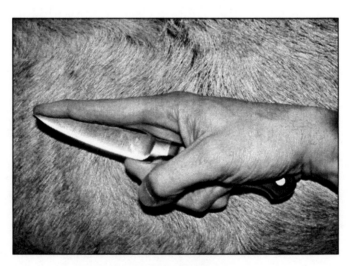

A good knife hold
to cut one layer of flesh at a time

Return to the bottom of the sternum and carefully nick the layer of muscle wall that is now exposed. Do not cut into the gut bag below it. If your knife has a gut hook, use the hook to slice the muscle wall open from the sternum down to the anus. If you do not have a gut hook, use your index finger once again to cover the tip of the blade and the spine. Slice the muscle wall with the blade facing upward. The white tissue you see below this muscle layer is the gut bag.

Slide your gloved hands through the opening and feel the exterior of the gut bag. You will find that there is connective tissue loosely attached to the bag all around its girth. The greatest amount of connective tissue is near the spine. Gently detach as much of this tissue as possible with your hands, and use the knife only if necessary.

The gut bag tapers down into the pelvis. Between the deer's hind legs, you will notice that there are larger vessels, a urethra and the colon descending into the pelvis. If you have a bone saw, carefully cut the pelvis open, right in the center. If you do not have a bone saw, core the anus from the outside with the knife and pull it up and out of the pelvis. The gut bag should now slide out of the animal but remain attached at the diaphragm. Puncture the diaphragm with your knife and reach as high as possible with one hand and pull a lung down. Slice the connection above the lung with the knife. Repeat this action for the other lung. Now do the same for the heart. Lastly, reach as high as you can and pull on the esophagus and windpipe. Slice the esophagus and windpipe with the knife and everything should now fall free of the animal. There will be a lot of blood here, especially if your shot passed through these vital organs.

You are almost done. The worst is over. Next—with your hands only—pull off any large pieces of fat resting against the lower portion of the spine. Be careful not to damage the tenderloins. If you are able, wash the cavity out with snow—or water if you are near a clean water source. If not, it is time to drag the animal out of the forest and do the washing at home.

Transporting your deer out of the woods can be a very strenuous activity. I don't own an ATV, and on occasion I have had to drag my deer as far as a quarter of a mile before getting to a road. Each time I endure a long drag like that I resolve to increase my exercise routine so I will be better prepared for the next season. I have been fortunate that my largest kills had to be hauled only short distances. But experience has taught me that pulling even a small deer can wear me out in fewer than 100 yards. If you do not prepare for a long drag, you will find that pulling a deer with your arms while walking backwards and juggling a gun or bow will be exhausting at best and impossible at worst. For this reason I carry 15 feet of ¾ inch diameter rope that I arrange so I can drag my deer while walking forward with my hands relatively free. Here is how to do it: With one end of the rope, tie a bowline knot around the base of the animal's antlers. At the other end, tie a second bowline big enough to put your chest and one shoulder through. A bowline knot is a loop that does not constrict when pulled. Be sure to learn how to make such a knot so that while pulling your deer, the loop will not tighten around your chest. If you have a doe, bring the forelimbs up to her head and tie the bowline around her neck and forelimbs. This rope method will make the best use of your strength and energy, especially when hauling a heavy deer. For at least part of the journey, you will likely have to drag your animal over some rocks and downed branches. Slow down over the rough terrain and do not jerk the rope too harshly. The meat can be easily bruised, and you don't want to damage what you have worked so hard for.

Once you have transported the deer to your vehicle, the next challenge is picking up the animal and loading it for the ride home. This is certainly easier when you have a friend with you or a hoist that can lift the deer. But if you are a solo hunter you need another approach. When I am alone, I lean two wooden planks on the tailgate of my pickup truck to form ramps that help me get the deer into the bed. I recommend using a pair of 2x8 boards about 8 feet long. Space the boards far enough apart so that you can walk between them. Slide the deer onto the ramps until they are supporting its weight. Walk between the planks while pushing the body up and onto the truck bed. This has worked for me with deer that weighed over 150 lbs. That might not sound very heavy, but once you try lifting a floppy dead animal into a truck bed, you will see just how cumbersome it can be.

My daughter Lauren helping me wash out a deer

Now you can head home right? Not necessarily. Depending on where you killed the deer, you will likely have to drive to the nearest check station first to fulfill several state requirements. In my state, an official will record certain data about the dead deer, and band it with a Massachusetts tag. Fortunately I have 48 hours so I can go home first with it. In Massachusetts and many other states you must keep the deer visible while being transported until the state band has been attached. If this is the case in your state keep the tail gate open or be sure a hoof sticks out somewhere. After you have complied with your state's laws, the deer is yours to do with as you please. I recommend that you cape it as soon as you get home to cool the meat further. Caping will be discussed in detail in the following chapter. But if you are exhausted from all the activity of the day, caping can be done later.

Before you call it a day, you need to hang the deer upside down in a cool garage or shed where predators and weather will not get at it. This allows residual blood to drain, aids in the cooling process while keeping the animal off of the dirt or floor. You will need a hoist or block and tackle, and a gambrel. These things can be made from parts purchased at your local hardware store or you can buy a kit from most sporting goods stores. The gambrel hooks into the deer's rear legs. There is a large tendon on each back leg that resembles a human Achilles tendon. Feel around it until you locate the thin section of flesh between the tendon and the larger portion of the leg. Cut a two-inch long slit behind the tendon in each leg and hook the gambrel through each opening. Now hoist the gambrel up until the deer is off the ground.

A light duty gambrel with a block and tackle

Ideally the temperature where you store the deer should be somewhere between 33-40 degrees F. If you have no choice but to allow the deer to freeze or go above 45 degrees, you will want to take some actions that we will address in the chapter "Come and Get It". But for now, you have probably done all you want to do with the deer for the day. Go take a well-deserved and much-needed shower.

# 14

# Come And Get It!
## (Caping, Aging, Cutting And Storing Your Meat)

$T$he following is a list of tools that I like to have for meat processing. I describe each item and their use within the chapter. These should be acquired and prepared before deer-hunting season. Please read through this chapter's instructions prior to attempting to process a deer. This will help you to plan ahead so you can have everything ready and in good working condition.

- ✓ gambrel with a block and tackle (the deer has been hanging on this from the previous chapter)
- ✓ freezer
- ✓ mechanical meat tenderizer
- ✓ sheltered work area
- ✓ 4'x6' old counter top to use as a cutting board and work bench (smaller is okay)
- ✓ disinfectant cleanser
- ✓ a stand to place the counter top onto

239

✓ butcher paper or vacuum sealer with bags

✓ knives

✓ sharpening stone

✓ meat grinder

✓ fine toothed saw (hack saw, bone saw or wood saw)

✓ three large bowls or buckets

✓ cooking twine

✓ friends to share a meal with

One of the wonderful things about hunting is the rewarding meals that follow! Seeing all the smiling faces around the table makes my heart sing. Sitting down to tenderloins, cutlets and stews, or meatloaf, hamburgers and sloppy "does" is a treat that can be enjoyed the whole year round. Free range and organic foods are not new ideas to hunters. Venison and other wild game epitomize those concepts. How ironic that many of today's self-appointed enlightened thinkers will eat only organic foods, and fail to realize they are "just catching up" to the huntsmen. If you are really concerned about hormones, antibiotics or preservatives, you can rest assured that wild game is entirely free of such questionable substances. And if you are a "do-it-yourselfer," not only will hunting excite you, but getting the meat to the table might be pleasing to you as well.

For years I hired professional meat cutters to cut and package my meat. One was a fellow who did the work in a shed behind his house. Year after year I would chat with him while he worked for hours on my deer. He enjoyed the company and answered all my questions as I watched his skillful hands working his knives and tying up roasts. Eventually he moved away, and I hired another fellow who didn't want any company while he worked. That left me feeling as though I was missing something. It just didn't seem right to drop the deer on his garage floor and return the following day to retrieve nicely packaged steaks and ground venison without having watched the process. My uncle Les suggested that I try butchering the next deer myself. And with his guidance, coupled with my years of watching a professional, we finished a deer together in about four hours. After cutting up countless more deer on my own, I now have enough experience and confidence to share with you what I know. We will start with aging and caping the deer. If you intend to have the head mounted, contact your taxidermist within 24 hours of the kill. He will give you instructions on how he wants the animal caped. Often taxidermists have a particular way they want the hide handled and they may want to cape the animal themselves. Don't be surprised if he wants you to bring the animal to him immediately. But if you are just going to eat the deer and don't intend to mount the head on the wall, you can follow my instructions for an easy way to cape it.

The first thing a hunter should know about processing meat is how to age it properly. I have read a variety of scientific and opinion articles on how to age meat, and over the years I have developed my own methods. They have been refined by my own mistakes and successes. One time I shot a yearling and cut it into steaks within a day. Surely a yearling would be tender right? Who needs to age that meat? But what a surprise to discover that when the meat was cooked it was tough and didn't taste very good. I learned a big lesson: never disregard the aging process. The difference between having fabulous meals or gamey shoe leather lies in how you handle your deer from forest to freezer. Thankfully, processing meat is not complicated. Let me save you some frustration and research.

Starting within an hour of the death of your deer, rigor mortis will set into the meat. After 24 hours this will subside. The meat will still be firm but the extreme tightness will have lessened. During this initial 24 hour period, do not begin the meat cutting. Just store the deer at a temperature between 33 and 45 degrees Fahrenheit. If you cannot keep the deer from freezing, then bring it into the basement of your house. If the temperature is too high, pack the deer with ice, inside and out. Cutting the deer during the first 24 hours will result in hard work and tough meat. Patience will reward you.

The aging process begins in earnest after rigor mortis has diminished. Enzymes and acids—primarily lactic acid—are present in meat. If a deer died quickly, its meat will contain significant levels of acid and very little adrenal hormone. People theorize that these biochemicals affect flavor. While that is yet to be proven, one thing is certain: lactic acid is your friend. It breaks down tough cell walls and collagen in the meat and tenderizes it for you.

Now let's be clear here. Allowing enzymes and acids to work on your meat is not the same as allowing bacteria to work on your meat.

Bacteria causes rot. It eats the meat and generates byproducts that stink. Enzymes and acids break down the meat in a good way. Thus, the aging process is simply allowing them to tenderize the meat. Although we cannot completely protect our meat from airborne bacteria and from contact with contaminated surfaces, we can inhibit bacterial growth by keeping the meat cold. As stated earlier, the ideal aging temperature is between 33 and 45 degrees Fahrenheit. At temperatures below freezing, bacteria won't grow, but enzymes and acids won't function either. When temperatures are above 45 degrees, bacteria grow rapidly and spoil meat quickly.

Much of the beef we purchase in supermarkets has aged a few days, and the results are great. Fine restaurants age their meat even longer to yield those sensational "cut-with-a-butter-knife" steaks.

Whether your deer is a yearling or an old buck with no teeth left, follow the same aging process. Assuming you can maintain the correct temperature, let the deer age for five days. If you cannot maintain the optimum cool range, and the temperature rises to 50 degrees, then age the deer for only three days. If you cannot prevent temperatures from getting higher than 50 degrees, then age it for only one day. Butchering the deer that early will yield less tender meat, but the bacteria will not have time to damage your prize.

For less than ideal circumstances I have a trick to share with you. If you must butcher the meat early because you cannot control the temperature, then cut it and vacuum seal it. Next, if you have the room, put all the meat into the refrigerator to age it there for a total of five days. The temperature is usually stable, and factory settings keep most refrigerators just above freezing. Place a thermometer in yours if you wish to make sure it is in the 33 to 45 degree range. After the five days of aging in the refrigerator, your vacuum sealed meat can be transferred to the freezer. You might want to put the tenderloins right into a marinade and enjoy a celebration dinner while the rest of your deer freezes.

You can age the meat longer than five days. Many people do. However, I do not like to risk possible bacteria growth, so I never age my deer beyond five days. While the aging process alone will sufficiently tenderize venison, you can achieve truly buttery-soft meat if you buy a mechanical tenderizer. This device comes in several styles such as a mallet or needle type. I recommend using the mechanical tenderizer just before you marinate your meat. These tenderizers are available at most hunting outfitters and kitchen supply stores.

As the deer is hanging in your cool garage at the ideal 40 degrees, you can get everything ready for cutting. Here is my favorite setup: a sheltered area with a comfortable temperature suited to the work — my garage. The job is messy, and if you don't finish after a few hours you will want to take a break and come back to it later. That makes the kitchen a poor choice and the basement less than ideal. A garage or shed that can be heated a bit is just right. Electricity is a bonus for working into the night, for running a vacuum sealer and for playing your favorite radio station while you work.

Get your hands on an old counter top. A plywood board is okay but tends to be damaged easily by the knives, making it almost impossible to remain sanitary. And even the largest cutting boards are not big enough for full length back straps and long limbs. Talk to some contactors or kitchen remodeling companies, and see if you can acquire a six foot long section of discarded counter top. This surface will stand up well to the knife for many years before wearing out. Next, find some folding legs for the counter top. Portable folding legs are made for contractors who need strong temporary workbenches on the job. The convenience is worth the price. You could also build your own set of legs or use saw horses. Personally I prefer to work while standing, so I set my surface height at 38 inches.

You will also need butcher paper or a vacuum sealer. Butcher paper is a very inexpensive option. I used butcher paper many times to wrap my meat. Then I tried a vacuum sealer, and I never went back to paper. The butcher paper occasionally allows blood to leak through and I can't stand that. Vacuum sealers are superior because the meat is preserved in a sealed, airtight bag that prevents leakage and freezer burn. And when you shop for a vacuum sealer, remember that you get what you pay for. A piston pump style will cost a bit more than the turbine style because it removes far more air. I recommend the piston pump.

My set of meat cutting knives

Now let us talk about knives. As I stated before, you can cut an entire deer into packaged steaks using any type of knife. However, your work will be easier and more efficient if you have the following: A stout two-inch blade for caping, a fine (short distance from spine to cutting edge) three-inch blade for cutting along the bones, a fine six-inch filet style knife for removing fascia and separating muscle groups, and a broad six-inch knife for slicing large muscle groups into steaks. The thinner the blades are the better. While this set is the ideal, you do not need all of these knives to properly butcher your venison. You can get away with fewer or even just one. However, be sure that any knife you use is as sharp as you can make it. The blade will be dulled before the job is complete.

Another important item to have on hand is a meat grinder. Good quality used meat grinders are available everywhere. When I was young I saw them at almost every yard sale. Now I look online for them and occasionally find even accessory meat grinders for electric mixers. The accessory-style meat grinder that attaches to the Power Take Off (PTO) of modern mixers is inexpensive and very powerful. If you have the strength and stamina you can certainly use a hand crank type. If you plan to keep butchering your own game and can afford a modern electric machine, by all means purchase a new one. It may be a good idea to borrow or rent a grinder for your first deer. If you find that you do not enjoy butchering your own deer, you will not have invested too much money. If you decide to buy a used grinder as I have, look for a refurbished unit. There is a potential downside with a used grinder: the condition of the knives and the dies. After years of service, knives need re-sharpening and dies need to be resurfaced. If a used grinder has not been refurbished you can handle the job yourself with a diamond sharpening stone that you probably have for your hunting knives. If you don't own a diamond stone, you can get reasonable results using 1200 grit or finer sand paper. Resurfacing and sharpening with sandpaper must be done on a very hard and smooth surface such as a block of steel or super flat ceramic surface. The diamond stone is already both hard and flat.

Observe the knife portion of the grinder. It will generally look like an "X" located just behind the die. When you remove the die the knife will usually fall right out. The blade edges that come in contact with the die are the ones that need to be gently slid in circular strokes on the diamond stone or the sandpaper. You might want to put a bit of WD-40 or light oil on the sandpaper for this. When these edges of the X are flat and sharp on the side, you are finished. Wash the X-knife and set it aside. The die must be flattened out the same way to eliminate any scoring that the knife may have created as it sliced along the surface. Sometimes you can just flip the die over and use the untouched side if the previous owner did not already do that. Polish each face of the die to a shiny finish, and then wash and dry it well. Reassemble the machine and your grinder is ready for business.

It's time to start caping the deer while it hangs on the gambrel by its rear legs. Begin with your very sharp 2-inch, stout blade. In order to peel the hide from the body, you will need to make a couple more cuts from the opening that you created where you eliminated the gut bag. It is important to minimize the amount of animal hair that gets separated from the hide with each cut. Deer hair has a tendency to get all over your meat, your clothing, and the floor. You won't be happy when it gets into the packaged meat or when your spouse sees you tracking it into the house. Therefore as you cut the hide, work the blade under skin and slice up to the surface. When cutting in this manner, the hair will not be damaged and it will stay connected to the hide. Trust me; it is worth the extra effort. The deer should still be hanging from the gambrel while you do the following work. Below are the steps to follow for caping your deer, assuming that you do not intend to have the head mounted:

- Cut the hide along the inside of each of the deer's rear legs, starting from the open cavity and ending at the ankle joint just above the gambrel.

- Cut the hide in a circle around the ankle joint on each leg.

- Make another cut along the underside of each of the front limbs using the same technique. Start at the cavity and work the cut, under the hide, from the chest to the armpit and down to the wrist joint on each side.

- Cut the hide in a circle around each wrist joint as well.

- Using just your fingers, begin peeling the hide away from the ankle joints.

- Continue peeling the hide down the legs until the tail is reached. Cut through the base of the tail between the lowest vertebra using a bone saw, wood saw or knife. If you wish to keep the tail portion of the hide, cut the hide down the underside of the tail. Continue peeling the hide until you have the hips and legs completely exposed.

- At this point peel the hide from the wrists and expose the forearms.

- Continue to pull the hide down from the hips and past the rib cage. As you remove more of the hide, roll it so the hair side is in your hands. The hair side is easier to tug than the slippery underside. You will find that the hide adheres a bit tighter as you approach the neck.

⊕ Continue to free the hide from the front limbs and the shoulders until all that is left to cape is the neck.

⊕ The hide adheres to the neck more tightly than any other place on the deer but you can get it off with patience. Your goal is to pull the hide down to the ears.

⊕ If the hide is getting too difficult to pull off by hand only, take your knife out and carefully touch the boundary between neck meat and hide while you pull.

⊕ Continue to pull downward on the hide and continue touching the blade of the knife against the ring formed around the neck where the hide joins the body. If you wish, you can also make a cut from the sternum up the neck to the throat.

⊕ Take a bone saw, wood saw or knife and find a place to pass the tool between vertebrae as high up against the skull as you can reach in order to take off the deer's head. Do not worry if you can't get right up to the highest vertebra. This is a really tough part of the deer caping, and you won't lose much meat if you cut a few vertebrae below the skull.

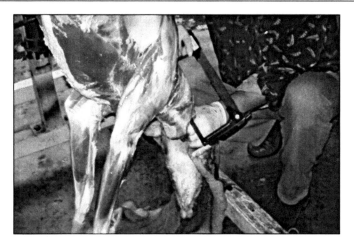

Cutting between the vertebrae close to the skull

⊕ At this point the deer's head and hide are removed leaving fur covered "socks" just above the hooves. To finish the caping, cut the hide around the base of the skull. You now have a complete hide removal, and you are ready to cut the meat! If you wish to save the hide, rub a pound of salt into it and roll it up. If you have the room, don't bother with the salt; just put it in a trash bag and freeze it.

⊕ Go wash up. Take a rest if you need it. Removing a hide is pretty physical work.

Let's take a moment to talk a bit about cleanliness. You will be taking out steaks, roasts and back straps, and grinding up meat. Your hands must be thoroughly washed and your work surfaces and tools disinfected. You don't need to get neurotic about cleanliness, but treat your work area as you would your own kitchen. Wear a baseball cap to keep your hair from falling on the food, and if you need to take a break to visit the bathroom or answer your phone, be sure to wash up completely before resuming work. Meat is a breeding surface for bacteria, so practice "the golden rule:" ensure the level of sanitation you would want the folks at restaurants and meat markets to use. Keep in mind that you will be serving this venison to people you know and love. Enough said.

It is virtually impossible to harvest a deer and not have a small amount of damaged or tainted meat. By tainted, I mean meat that has gone bad for some reason. You are probably familiar with the smell of fresh meat from the grocery store. It has a mild, yet appetizing odor even when raw. The same should be true for most of your venison. With every kill you will encounter some meat on the deer that has been bruised, either from impact with the ground at death or from dragging the animal over a rock while pulling it out of the forest. You certainly will find some of this damaged meat where your projectile struck or passed through the deer. Damaged venison will be either darker red or a shade of purple, and it will smell different from the good meat. If you spot meat that has an irregular color, put your nose to it. If it smells odd or displeasing, take one of your fine knives and slice away a few millimeters from the surface. Is it better looking below? Smell it again. Is it bruised all the way through? Maybe the discoloration was only superficial contamination from a pool of blood or other contaminant that sat on the surface of the meat too long. Meat that is damaged from non-bacterial contaminants will taste bad although it won't make you or your guests sick. Some folks who are trying venison for the first time might think the unpleasant taste is normal, and others might be too polite to tell you that your dinner tastes like a sweaty athletic sock. This is why I always tell my guests up front that if the meat does not taste really good, stop and take another piece.

Unlike beef, which has intramuscular fat, venison has extramuscular fat. This makes your job easier because you can safely cut away all the fat that you see and know that you are not wasting good meat. For the sake of completeness, let me remind you that fat is the white or yellow puffy flesh that can sometimes be very firm in texture on a deer. Fat deposits are the deer's fuel stores for winter. Most autumn-harvested deer will have some. Unlike beef fat and pork fat, deer fat tastes terrible. Therefore cut all of it away when you encounter it.

Fascia is another tissue you will encounter. Fascia is a smooth membrane that surrounds muscle groups and allows the muscles to slip past each other as they work. It is clear to translucent, but in thicker areas it will appear white. Fascia does not taste bad, but it is difficult to chew when it is thick. No matter how long you chew it, it will never break down. Fascia therefore should be removed during the cutting process. Its removal can be a bit time consuming but well worth the effort. You will see fascia surrounding almost every muscle. Slide your thin knife under it. If you can still see the knife blade through the fascia, you are doing great. If the knife disappears below the meat, you are slipping it too deeply into the flesh. After you properly insert the knife under the membrane, slide the blade along the boundary between the meat and the fascia to separate them. Take your time. Frankly, the professional wild game meat-cutters will not spend enough time and energy on this. They are trying to make money and fascia-removal is considered an efficiency killer. They would rather let you slice away this membrane just before you cook your meat. When doing your own butchering you can choose to remove fascia either before packaging or before cooking. I prefer to do it before packaging.

Tendon is the tough white cord that connects the muscles to the bones. It is inedible and should not remain attached to the meat. Don't put it into the meat grinder either because it will bind up your machine. The Native Americans used it very effectively for cordage.

Meat cutting on my work bench

You can watch videos and read books on how to become a meat-cutter. After all, it is a profession and requires training and skill. What I am going to teach you will make most professional meat-cutters say: "That guy is an amateur." And they would be right. After all, an amateur is someone who is not paid to do the work that they do. But don't let my lack of formal training scare you away from this work. The concepts and processes I am about to share are quite simple and effective. Our great-great-great-grandfathers cut deer, and they did just fine without a lot of formal training or even the internet!

🍴 Set up three large bowls or clean plastic buckets. One will be for the meat that will be ground into burger. Another will be for steaks and tips. The third will be for discarded bones, tendons, fascia, fat and damaged meat. Place these buckets beside your work bench. As we go along, I will be telling you what meat to put into each bucket. The burger bucket will double as the stew meat bucket. I don't cut any of my venison into stew meat. In my opinion the tougher meat— as well as odds and ends that are too small to be steak tips—should just become burger. When my wife and I want to make a stew, we use good quality steaks and cut them into bite-size pieces.

🍴 The first steaks to remove are the two tenderloins. As their name suggests, these are tender cuts. They are shaped like trout—narrow and tapered on each end, and are located just above the pelvis on both sides of the spine. To remove them, begin with just your fingers. Slide your fingers along each side of the spine, separating every muscle from the surrounding tissue and backbone. Use your fine three-inch blade if necessary. In this location, it is acceptable to cut a bit of extra flesh surrounding the tenderloins and then trim the excess fat later when the meat is on the bench. Slice away the damaged or discolored meat, and place these two tender strips of prime venison into your steak bucket.

Rotate the carcass so that you are looking at the deer's back. There will be a fair amount of white, hard fat here. With your knife, trim the fat that comes off easily, being careful not to cut into the meat. Your goal is to be able to see the back strap, ribs and spine reasonably well for the next steps. While you will probably have no difficulty identifying the ribs and spine, you might be less familiar with the back straps—a pair of muscles that reside on each side of the spinal column, right up against the rib cage. They run from the shoulders down to the hips. Back straps are excellent meat, and I often cook them up on the grill when I have a lot of company. After grilling I slice them into 3/4 inch thick medallions.

To extract the back straps use a fine knife. Hold the carcass steadily with one hand while using your other hand to make this cut. Insert the blade into the middle of the back just to the left of the spine. Slide the knife in so that the blade separates the bone and meat. Depending on the size of the deer, the blade will go in only a couple of inches before it hits the rib cage. When you feel the knifepoint touch a rib bone, move the blade down along the spine maintaining constant contact with it. I actually cock the blade slightly so it scrapes along the spine while the tip drags along the rib cage until I reach the shoulder. Make this same cut upwards toward the hips. Now come around the top of this muscle where it ends at the hip and begin moving the knife down the body again, except this time, keep the blade point perpendicular to the spine and slide the cutting edge along the rib cage. Often the back strap will begin to fall out under its own weight. Again, if you over cut a bit, that is ok. There will be a lot of fascia and fat to remove from this long length of meat.

🍴 Repeat the steps above for the other side of the spine. After cleaning off all of the undesired materials, place these long strips of meat into the steak bucket.

🍴 Pull the left front limb away from the body a bit to identify where the foreleg muscles separate from the chest. Work your knife gently into the "armpit" along the boundary between the muscle groups. The front limb's connective tissue should be easy to cut because it is not like a human limb that contains a ball joint. Instead the scapula floats on the side of the rib cage bound by several muscle groups. Although hidden under muscle, it is part of the forelimb. Following the clear boundary between the chest and the front limb, move your knife between the chest and the arm muscle group until the limb falls away. Carry this limb to the work bench.

You should now have a limb on the bench comprised of a hide-covered hoof to the wrist joint, a forearm, an upper arm and a scapula. The limb's bones are hidden under the muscles, but it should be obvious where they are. Do not try to separate the bones at the joints. That is both difficult and unnecessary. Instead, begin by sliding a long thin blade along the scapula, pulling the muscle away from the bone. Clean off undesirable materials from the leg venison. Some people cut the limb muscles into stew meat, but I prefer to put them in the burger bucket and grind them up.

After the muscles are cut away from the scapula bone, look to the other side of the joint just below the scapula and carefully work your knife down the bone of the arm, separating the muscle from the bone. Remove inedible material and place the meat in the burger bucket. Separate the muscles of the forearm from the bone as you did with the upper portion of the limb. Again, remove and discard the tendons and fascia of which there will be an abundant amount. Put the meat into the burger bucket.

Repeat the above operation for the other front limb.

Personally I think the meat between the ribs and the thin meat layers just outside the rib cage that are equivalent to flank steaks should be put into the burger bucket for grinding. I have tried slow cooking, brining and smoking deer ribs. Yet for all that effort, the results have not been nearly as tender and delicious as pork ribs. Nevertheless if you wish to cook up the ribs, take a hack saw or a reciprocating saw and cut the rib cage as close to the spine as possible on each side. If you have a very large animal you can break up the rack or cut through the middle of each row of ribs again. I recommend slow-cooking the rib meat all day in a crock pot with a lot of barbeque sauce.

🍴 Next, take a saw and cut between the vertebrae as close to the pelvis as possible. Lay the spine and neck down in a clean spot. Later we will put it on the bench to take out the neck roast.

🍴 Make a vertical cut through the pelvis so that the two rear legs are separated. At this point the rear legs will be balanced on the gambrel, so be careful that they don't fall off. I recommend you take one off and lay it safely with the neck you set aside; place the other leg onto the work bench.

🍴 Usually the leg meat closest to the pelvis will have become dried and dark. I routinely shave off a couple of millimeters from the surface of this section. Maneuver the limb until you can locate the socket where the leg connects to the pelvis. Slide your knife toward this joint, carefully following the boundaries between the many large muscle groups in the haunch. As you get closer to the joint, cut the tendons and ligaments binding the ball to the pelvis. Throw the half pelvis into the discard bucket.

Now take a look at this upper hind leg. You will see many muscle groups intertwined together. Don't panic. Work your fingers and knife along the boundaries between muscle groups until they separate. Next, slide the knife carefully around the bone and free the muscles completely. Clean off the fascia, tendons and fat and place the venison in the steak bucket. Later we will cut those muscle bundles finer. Be aware that there is a tarsal gland in each rear leg that belongs in the discard bucket. Located near the joint that points backwards, the gland looks very strange and not like something you would want to eat. Years ago when I was a less-educated hunter, I thought it was a blood clot, but at least I knew it was not edible.

Now run your knife along the bone of the lower leg taking care not to cut into the muscle. Try just to separate the muscle from the bone. This portion will have a lot of tendon, sinew and fascia. Cut away these undesirable parts and put them in the discard bucket. Place the good muscle in the steak bucket.

Repeat the above for the second rear leg.

The neck has many muscle bundles surrounding the spine and windpipe. These enable the deer to move its neck in a wide range of positions and directions. It would take quite a lot of effort to separate the muscle groups and clean them all. So here are two culinary options for the neck meat that will not require as much removal of inedible material at this stage. I choose either to create a large neck roast or to put the neck in the burger bucket. If you have the time and the desire, give the neck roast a try. Begin by cutting between two vertebrae as low to the shoulder as you can. Leave the neck bones in the roast, but try to remove the esophagus, which looks like a thick vein, and the wind pipe which looks like a rigid, ringed tube that does not collapse upon itself. Wrap the neck in cooking twine and set it aside for packaging. If you do not want to make a roast out of the neck, you still must remove the wind pipe and esophagus before you carefully cut away all of the meat from the vertebrae and put it in the burger bucket.

Take a moment now to carefully go over all the bones and remove any other meat that can be placed into the burger bucket. Most of what is left on the carcass now is undesirable.

Clear your work bench of blood, bits of meat and maybe even some deer hair. Sanitize the surface well and dry it off. Take all the venison out of the steak bucket and lay it on the bench. What follows is my favorite part of the meat-cutting job! The steak bucket contents are tender enough to be served as steaks and roasts, and now can be cut and packaged accordingly.

I suggest starting with the back straps. Often I will take these roughly two-foot-long steaks, cut them in half and package them separately. This way I don't have to thaw too much meat

261

at one time. But if you expect to have a big barbeque with a lot of friends, it is a real treat to pull out one whole side of back strap for such an event. Some people cut the entire back strap into cutlets between one half and one inch thick. This is another great option. With two large back straps, you can try a combination of things. Once you have cut them as desired, leave them on the table for vacuum sealing.

Next, find the football-shaped steaks from each rear upper leg. These can be tied up with cooking twine. If you choose to keep them whole as a roast, be sure to use cooking twine and not some odd twine from your garage. But I prefer to cut these into one-inch-thick steaks and set them aside. Because the muscle is football-shaped, its ends will be odd-sized pieces of meat. These are steak tips! Put these tips in a dedicated spot on your table for all the steak tips you will encounter in the steps to follow.

Move onto the next big muscle. Look at the meat and determine at what angle you should cut to produce the greatest number of nicely-shaped large steaks. I like to cut my steaks one-inch thick, but you can certainly slice them thinner. Thicker steaks tend to stay juicier when grilled. Another consideration before cutting up the large muscle is the grain. The grain refers to muscle fibers that are visible and run in a clear direction. Always cut your steaks perpendicular to the grain. This makes for easier chewing as well as more effective marinating and seasoning. Again, after you have cut all your steaks out of the larger piece of meat, put the small, leftover chunks in the steak tip pile.

🍴 Continue cutting until you have finished all the meat in the bucket. Group your steaks into sizes and amounts that best fit your family. That way you can defrost one package per meal and more packages as needed when guests are over for dinner.

🍴 Vacuum seal the groups. Then label and date the packages.

🍴 Grind up all the meat pieces in the burger bucket and vacuum seal them in one pound packages. Label and date these too.

🍴 Ground venison does not need to be aged, so the burger packages should be frozen right away to keep them as bacteria free as possible. The steak packages can be temporarily stored in the refrigerator if you intend to age your meat longer. Otherwise just put them directly into the freezer.

🍴 Clean up!

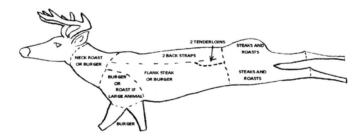

A basic meat cutting diagram

If you are a coyote hunter as I am, you may wish to keep your discarded meat and bones for coyote bait. Check with your local game laws. To dispose of this material, it is best to dump it deep in the forest where it will be eaten quickly by raccoons, coyotes, fishers and other nocturnal animals as well as crows by day. If that is not convenient for you, place it in strong trash bags and put it with your household trash. You must be hungry by now. Go eat those tenderloins!

Many people ask me for venison recipes. Most beef recipes will work well for venison without alteration if you keep in mind that it is leaner than beef. For those few recipes that do require a higher fat content olive oil or egg can be added as substitutes for the missing fat. Some people even buy fat and inject it. I prefer not to go that route. To make venison hamburgers or meatballs, it will be necessary to add something to help the meat stick together. Put one egg in every pound of burger for those applications. When I prepare steaks for the grill, I always use olive oil in the marinade. This will stop the charring that can happen when low fat meat is placed on a hot cooking surface. Although deer burger should be cooked to the "well done" state, the steaks can be cooked rarer than ground meat because they are inherently more sanitary. If cooked too long, venison steaks will quickly become tougher than beef steaks. Rare and medium rare steaks will be your best bet.

If you really want recipes specific to venison, the internet is full of them. The most common and simple recipe I use for my steaks is this: Place a couple of steaks in a plastic container with an air tight lid and drizzle olive oil all over them. Season both sides of the steaks with garlic salt and let them sit for a few hours. With the grill

at about 350 degrees, cook your steaks until they are medium rare.
That takes about five minutes or less on each side for ¾ or one-inch
steaks. Give thanks and eat up!

Back strap with a spice rub

 **15**

# Your Footprint Is Beautiful
## (Forest And Game Management Through Enhancement And Harvesting)

*J*umping Badger was a ten year old Native American. His family and tribe had taught him many skills. Jumping Badger was an eager student who excelled at all the basics such as finding clean water, building durable shelters and making fire. He spent his evenings bone-carving with his friends. Much of his day was spent with White Feather, the medicine woman who taught him how to wisely choose the animals to bring home. Because Jumping Badger was rapidly maturing and was well-respected, Grandfather Sitting Bear had great confidence that he was ready to go away by himself for a while to complete his journey into manhood. And so, one evening the boy was given a departing ceremony followed by a time in the sweat lodge with his family and elders. Then Jumping Badger was sent off into the night. He would return after a full cycle of the moon.

At the end of a day's journey, Jumping Badger built a shelter in a suitable place. The second day he set a long string of small animal traps that he could visit each day to collect what he had snared. And he built a second shelter just beyond the last trap. Each morning he would walk the trap line and gather the captured critters. He picked wild edible plants as well. This effort guaranteed a satisfying dinner every evening. After a couple of days of work, all his basic needs were filled and Jumping Badger now had free time to think and reflect. He began to wonder what gifts he should bring home for his grandfather, his mother and the elders of the tribe. Being a gifted bone-carver, he decided to create some beautiful knife handles and jewelry. He had found some chert stone that he would knap into blades for the knives. If he could acquire some large bones or antlers he could begin his projects.

Remembering the teaching of White Feather, Jumping Badger spent the next seven days watching a herd of deer that visited a meadow every morning and evening. White Feather had taught the boy to observe the habits, personality, strengths and weaknesses of each deer in order to select the right one to take home. Any deer could provide the strong sinew along each side of the spine for a great bow string. Each had a good hide that could be made into clothing and pouches. Each had bones that could be formed into tools and each had wonderful meat for meals. However, the boy needed to choose the animal that would not only serve him, but also benefit the herd by its loss. This dual stewardship required careful observation, thought and patience.

Jumping Badger noted that the small herd of deer entered the meadow from the same trail every morning. So he climbed a tall pine tree at the end of the trail and quietly watched the group of two bucks and three does come and go just below him. One evening he pulled a chunk of bark from the tree and playfully dropped it onto a doe's head as the group paused at the mouth of the trail. The doe startled and bumped into each of her friends as she attempted to escape. They ran in a circle, spooking the bucks that then darted down the trail back toward the forest, only to stop and look back wondering what the trouble had been. Jumping Badger had to trill like a red squirrel to cover his uncontainable laughter.

That night as Jumping Badger sat beside the glowing embers of his cooking fire, he recalled how the deer had been startled. He had noticed that one of the does, upon being spooked, had run in a circle on only three of her legs. One of her rear legs was not used and he wondered why. Tired, he began to doze. The proverbs of White Feather echoed in his mind. "Take with thanksgiving, and take only what you need. Take with others' needs in mind, and leave the herd and others better for it." The following evening Jumping Badger was back in the pine tree by the trail as the little herd of deer came through. He was surprised at their predictability. Usually he had to work much harder to identify habits in the deer he hunted with his grandfather. He looked for the deer that ran on only three legs. But all the deer were walking normally. This time Jumping Badger hurled a carved Oak stick at the lead buck's antlers and struck them perfectly. The buck turned and ran out of the path and into the thicket where he stood and looked back at buck number two.

The second buck was not startled, but the does ran back up the trail a short distance before turning to see what had caused the false alarm again. Jumping Badger could see that when one of the does ran, she did not lower her right rear leg. She used the leg normally to walk but not to run. This deer clearly could not escape danger as fast as her companions. She would fall soon to a predator. Jumping Badger was pleased. He now knew he had found the deer he would harvest.

Although this book is about deer hunting, I think it is important to explain briefly how the ideals of environmental enhancement and herd management should be an integral part of man's interactions with wildlife. I hold this view for two reasons:

- First, I have indicated throughout this book that I believe God commands us to be wise stewards of His creation (Genesis 1:28-30). This stewardship encompasses everything from the smallest wild edible plants to the largest trees, from tiny chipmunks to big game animals. In addition to providing us with plant and animal populations sufficient for our food, clothing and shelter, God has made these broadly reproducible to sustain mankind in perpetuity. Therefore out of my accountability to God and my love for my fellow man, I believe I have a responsibility to utilize nature in proportion to my needs and not to wantonly destroy it.

- Second, whether in our back yards, the town forest or the deeper wilderness, we can actually make wildlife healthier, stronger and more abundant by carefully choosing what we take and how we take it. In fact we can foster these improvements much faster than if we were to leave the woodland to take its own natural course. That's right. Biological science has affirmed that we can mature and improve the health of a forest and its inhabitants faster than would occur naturally. The key is knowledge and its consistent proper application. Many people stumble over this idea and insist that we should just leave the woods and the animals alone. Perhaps they do not understand man's place in relation to nature. Or maybe they have seen too many of man's destructive mistakes. Whatever their reasons for their views, these well-intentioned people who care about nature usually do not understand wildlife management. But given the right instruction, people who want to preserve the natural world can be taught to do great good.

How do we effectively steward the land? In the opening story of Jumping Badger, we learned that harvesting a weaker deer for man's use will also benefit the herd while sparing the weak animal from the suffering of a prolonged violent death through a natural predator. A similar principle applies to the plant kingdom as well. Here is one relatable example. Suppose we enter the woods to gather firewood early in the year so it can be cut, split and dried for the coming winter. How we can do it and leave the forest healthier, stronger, more mature and conducive to supporting more wildlife? Our little plot of woodland contains a range of growth from saplings to 50-year-old-trees. There is an abundance of red oak, a lesser amount of maple, a few beeches, a couple of hickory trees, a sparse amount of sassafras and absolutely no white oak. I am partial to white oak because the acorns are big, beautiful, and quite edible without much preparation. More importantly, these acorns are a staple for many forest dwellers from deer to squirrels. Consequently a large portion of white oak nuts are consumed before they have an opportunity to germinate. But we'll be able to do something about the lack of deer-attracting white oaks, as I'll explain shortly. There are also numerous standing dead trees, and although it seems logical to take those for firewood, there will be an even better source available to us if we refrain. Dead trees are full of bugs, thus providing food for birds, other reptiles and mammals. If they have become hollow due to decay, they also provide shelter and become dens.

Overhead the canopy is thick. The trees are spindly and closely competing. This is a characteristic of a young or immature forest. Years ago many saplings sprouted at the same time after the land was clear cut. As a result, the trees shot up to get the sunlight and did not grow as full and wide they would have if they germinated at different times. There is not much variation in their sizes: most are approximately one foot in diameter and about 50 feet tall. Some are very close together. Their dense canopy prevents most sunlight from reaching the forest floor. Consequently, the understory consists primarily of sparse blueberry bushes, and the ground is covered with leaves. Out of all the forest trees, the abundant red oak is an excellent slow-burning hard wood and a great choice for our needs. But we might notice that a couple of red oaks are leaning substantially. In fact, one is leaning so much it can barely reach the top of the canopy. It also is shading a large portion of the understory. That oak would be a great candidate for harvesting. Looking further, we see another red oak that has been struck by lightning and is split almost the whole way down the middle. As with the lame deer in the story of Jumping Badger, selecting weaker oaks will allow the stronger ones to thrive. Therefore after checking that they do not support nests, we should cut down those two trees that are destined to die early and are stunting the growth of the plants around them. This is preservation-friendly thinking. But let's not stop there.

After we have removed the trees, we can rake the forest floor where the sun now reaches the ground because we have created an opening in the canopy. By clearing away the leaves and roughing up the soil here, we will encourage the growth of seeds that are waiting underground for an opportunity to sprout. We can also transfer and plant some of the nuts found under the few hickory and beech mother trees. And if we have the time and energy, we can go to the neighboring forest populated with desirable white oaks and gather up a bunch of their acorns. Yes, their acorns can be hard to find since they are so sweet and delectable, but it takes only one to make a tree. We can bring those white oak acorns back to our little manmade plot in the forest and plant them as well. Would this kind of diversification and maturing of the forest happen naturally? Sure. Weaker trees will die eventually leaving the ground exposed. Birds and squirrels will possibly carry white oak nuts into the area. But we have sped up the process considerably and intelligently, not waiting on a slow and somewhat random system. The wild animals in the area will thrive on the changes. Our posterity will be very pleased. A mature forest will have more diverse plant life and support higher animal populations.

An avid hunter, and author of Whitetail Gardening: A Look at Micro-Food Plots, Vaughn Perkins takes the woodland gardening to another level. In his book, he describes ways to provide food plots to support whitetail deer and other critters on a larger scale. Vaughn points out that today's residential neighborhoods are often developed in areas once covered by large expanses of forest. Not all the wildlife is pushed out as we move in, and the little wooded parcels that remain are irregular shapes like jigsaw puzzles abutting homeowner properties. Therefore modern forest management must be adjusted to support wildlife within smaller woodland patches. Perkins' work teaches a form of wildlife gardening that creates micro-plots of specific food sources to address this issue. He goes further to show how to create cover not only for just deer, but for turkey as well. It is an enlightening, practical book that I heartily recommend for hunters.

Managing populations of large game animals such as deer is a bit more complicated than managing plant life. In my state, the Massachusetts Department of Fish and Game carries out this responsibility. The state biologists study many factors that make up a healthy herd such as the deer habitat. The land naturally limits how many deer it can support before food becomes scarce due to over browsing. Biologists also collect data on populations of coyotes and other predators in order to track the survival rates of fawns and mature deer. Reports from these state employees are generated every year and are posted online for public access. The number of buck and doe permits issued to hunters is adjusted annually to maintain or meet goals for herd size and ratios of male to female deer. Although we hunters are not directly involved in the decision-making at that level, we are the greatest asset in the state's deer management tool chest. Thankfully, we also benefit from the system. Simply put, the state manages the herd at a macro level and we hunters are the agents licensed to harvest the deer for our use. It was the hunters who established the game management system a few generations ago. But as government has become larger and more complex, individual hunters no longer work at the macro level. However, as I'll explain on the next page, hunters still can make good micro-level harvesting decisions that improve the quality of local herds.

How does the state make its macro-level decisions about wildlife management? To answer this, I'll use the example of optimal herd size. Only does produce offspring, and one buck can impregnate many does. Therefore, if the state's goal for the year is to increase the number of deer in a herd, then the harvesting of more bucks will be encouraged by the permit ratio. And harvesting mature bucks will increase food resources for the whole herd. Conversely, if the herd is overpopulated, more does should be harvested. Taking a doe eliminates at least one fawn and sometimes two in the spring.

The government wildlife agency also subdivides a state into multiple geographic zones that are grouped according to their shared characteristics: rural or urban, similar landscapes or deer populations. Then the agency regulates how many bucks and does may be harvested in each particular zone. The state's macro-level decision-making might extend to regulating the types of guns and ammunition used during hunting season to ensure people's safety or to protect drinking water sources from contamination.

Motivated hunters can enhance the state's efforts by practicing micro-level wildlife management. This does require study of the local herd and personal discipline in order to identify which deer is the best candidate for harvesting. I have been impressed at how well this micro-level management has been exercised on private game preserves where owners have great personal interest in a healthy herd. But for the rest of us who rely on state forests, it is challenging to find the time to become familiar with a local deer population. It is even more difficult to willingly pass up a great opportunity to shoot a random deer instead of tracking a management-minded target. This situation is exacerbated late in the season if the freezer still has no deer meat in it!

Quite honestly, the micro-level management methods I will describe on the next page do not happen often, if at all, in modern hunting scenarios. With today's busy schedules, it can be difficult to get out for just one day and hunt the nearest deer, let alone study the entire herd for weeks. I admit I have rarely spent enough time studying deer even though I employ trail cameras to aid in my observations while I am at work or sleeping. But the ideals of wild-life stewardship are still important and worth aiming for even if we fall short. Remember this simple principle even when it is difficult to achieve: Take from the herd in such a way as to leave it stronger as a result.

Nature itself continuously carries out micro-level management of the herd. Unfortunately nature's way is very slow and harsh. For instance, during a hard winter with deep snow and scarce food, all the deer will become weak. To conserve their energy, they will move as little as possible waiting for spring to return. The fittest animals will survive the strong cold winds, storms and snow. But many of the weaker ones will die of exposure to the elements or from starvation. Predators—usually coyotes—will kill others. Because the coyotes too are trying to conserve their energy, they prey on the feeblest deer which are easiest to catch. Did the coyote do a good job "managing" the herd? In this case, yes. After all, there will be more food for the stronger, healthier survivors as a result of removing the weaker deer. Hardier genes will also be passed on to the next generation. This may sound a bit "Darwinian." The weaker animals will be eliminated naturally, often through a slow and painful death. Man, on the other hand, can move the process along faster and with less suffering–intelligently–in reflection of his God-given dominion over creation.

Most of the time nature's course will result in a stronger herd, but not always. I witnessed a situation through which the natural process took a devastating turn. One winter three feet of snow accumulated in the forest. There was a big thaw one day followed by a refreeze the following night resulting in the top layer of snow becoming hard crust. The coyotes easily ran over the top of the snow the next time they visited the deer herd. But the deer with their pointy hooves and heavier girth broke through the crust and sank in the snow up to their bellies as they tried to move about. They had to expend a tremendous amount of energy to take each step and could not achieve the speed necessary to escape danger. The coyotes had no challenge running down and eating any deer they wished. In fact, because a coyote's instinct is to kill the easy prey, and the deer were all helpless, the pack killed more deer than they could eat. The entire herd was nearly destroyed in two days even though most of the deer were left uneaten. This shows that the natural process has some variables in it that might generate undesired results. The following hunting season almost no doe tags were distributed, and buck tags were issued sparingly.

Thinking back to the story of Jumping Badger, consider the ideal scenario where a modern deer hunter has the time to study the condition of the deer in the herd individually. He selects the best deer to take in order to benefit the rest of the herd. That could be a very large buck among a high concentration of mature ones in a small area where scarce food is causing damaging competition. Another candidate for harvest is a deer with a weakness such as a health problem or a genetic disorder. Many health anomalies are easy to see such as a limp resulting from an improperly healed broken bone. Numerous other visible injuries are caused by nonlethal auto collisions or coyote encounters. Genetic disorders manifest noticeably with symptoms such as deformed antlers or piebald. Some states prohibit the hunting of piebald deer. Yet these animals have significant defects such as an overarched spine, short legs and a poorly formed jaw resulting in an under bite. Protecting them begs the question; "Is that hunting regulation likely to improve the herd or is that regulation based on emotion and more likely to harm the herd?" Some states are home to deer with health problems such as "Blue Tongue," a viral infection that makes the animals lethargic. This ailment is common in livestock and is harmless to humans who eat the infected meat. Venison tainted with Blue Tongue is likewise considered safely consumable. Even so, I do not recommend eating diseased deer. However shooting an afflicted deer will surely slow the spread of the problem.

In an ideal world, after studying and processing all the information before him, the hunter will pursue the deer that he believes will benefit the herd best by its absence. Additional time and effort will be expended to secure an opportunity to actually shoot that particular animal. How realistic is that? Well, to the weekend warrior who has only a limited time to spend on his hobby, it is not realistic at all. Let us be candid. You want a big set of antlers on your wall. And you want a freezer packed with meat. Rest easy, because a really healthy herd can tolerate a lack of quality micro-level management. The good news is that deer herds close to rural neighborhoods are nearly always quite overpopulated! That's right. Deer numbers are rapidly increasing, especially near thickly settled residential neighborhoods. Usually I obtain a minimum of two doe permits annually and fill at least one if not both. Statistics indicate that deer populations near humans are greater per square mile than they are in the deep wilderness. Therefore you will not need to observe every deer within a ten-mile radius in order to decide which animal to shoot for micro-level herd management. In all my years of hunting, every deer I have ever harvested has been taken within a quarter mile of a neighborhood or behind my own home. During some years, extreme natural conditions may greatly reduce deer numbers. In such circumstances every hunter's micro-level herd management will matter more. Even if you can't do it all, a small amount of responsible stewardship will ensure that your posterity will enjoy deer and other wildlife because your involvement is truly beneficial.

# 16

# Please Don't Hate Me
## (Public Relations)

"**D**on't you have anything better to do!", screamed an older woman with white hair, who didn't look strong enough to be generating such a loud voice. I was startled. Having just spent the last few hours still hunting, my buddy Mike and I were walking out of the forest making small talk and joking about how the deer must have all been in the next county for the morning. Our attention was on each other and the beautiful day. We approached Mike's van with our bows swinging at our sides. We kicked leaves and laughed like school boys do on a Friday afternoon. Our joy was shattered by the scowl on this poor woman's face while she stood strangely close to Mike's vehicle. "Why can't you leave the poor deer alone?! What have they ever done to you?!" Spit flew from her lips as her words, as sharp as our arrow heads, were calculated to inflict the most damage possible on our upbeat spirits. We were quite taken aback. Although we had both experienced encounters with people who do not approve of hunting, this incident was the worst ever. Mike wished the woman a good morning as he unlocked his van. I lifted the bow from my sling to put it away when I noticed that the woman had her right hand hidden behind her as she stepped backward away from us. My eyes narrowed as I looked at her carefully so I could remember her face. She continued to walk backwards, putting distance between us quickly. Then she spun around to walk forward down the road managing to keep her right hand out of sight.

This woman raised my suspicions. The previous season, I had hunted this spot and parked my car in this very same location. When I returned to the car to head home, I discovered that the silver paint had been gouged with some sort of a metal tool. The left side of my car, from the front fender, across both doors to the rear fender had a large swirling gouge in the paint. Until this point I had no idea who had done the dastardly deed. But now I believed I was looking at the culprit. I immediately walked around Mike's van to see if he had fallen prey to a similar act of vandalism. He had not. We likely came out of the forest at just the right time to save Mike from the expense and angst that I went through one year earlier. I am thankful that people like this are few and far between.

Hunting near neighborhoods means that you will interact with people far more often than you will in the deep woods. There are folks who jog or walk their dogs through the local woodlands. There will be people on the access roads as well. In some areas, you must pass through private property to enter a forest. It is important to seek permission from the owner to traverse private land or hunt directly on it. Property owners always deserve your respect, even if they refuse your request. When we sportsmen interact with people, we represent ourselves not only as benevolent members of society, but also as a responsible group of citizens–hunters. How we behave will impact how other hunters will be viewed. Give them a display of character that is beyond reproach and is above most standards of proper behavior. By doing this your conscience will be clear regardless of outcome because you are doing what is right.

Thankfully, the majority of folks I encounter are great people who are respectful, and they understand that hunting is legal, ethical and a positive use of one's discretionary time. Unfortunately, as my story with Mike showed, there are a few folks who believe hunters are the most heartless individuals to walk the planet since Charles Manson. Be mentally and emotionally prepared to face these people with the same love and respect as you do your grandfather. That's a tough one to practice, isn't it? Being loving and respectful does not mean you must agree with people who are wrong, nor does it mean you must stand there and take abuse. It means you should treat all people as you would want to be treated. Do your best to avoid abuse, and get out of bad situations. Never retaliate. Legal options are available to us if real harassment or damage to person or property occurs. Let the law handle that. Return a gentle answer. This type of response will sear the conscience of an attacker, and if there is any softness in his heart at all, he won't be able to live with how he treated such a kind and gentle person.

Whether in the forest or at your parking place, whether wearing camouflage or blaze orange, it is clear to everyone that you are an armed hunter. We owe it to the non-hunters to make them feel comfortable. Remember that our society is wary of anyone who has a bow or gun in their hand and a big fixed blade knife on their hip. So when you see other folks, be sure to smile. Say "Good morning!" to the woman walking down the access road with her dog, and "Hello!" to the jogging couple. This eases their minds and assures them that you are benevolent. I know that hunters are often in a rush to get to the woods, but it will generate good will to pause and say things such as "What a beautiful day to be out here!" or "That is a good-looking dog. Enjoy your walk!" You may sound unsophisticated, but you will have just changed the other person's perception of you from a possible maniac to a teddy bear.

Sometimes I have seen people on horseback, or walking or jogging through the forest. If they are not likely to notice you, just let them pass without disturbing them. However, if you are likely to be spotted, put your gun over your shoulder or your bow to your side. Again, smile and tip your hat. Exchange a few words and then turn back to your business. Trust me, it is the best way to engage people and leave them comfortable. Non-hunter encounters in the forest are rare and will vary depending on the location. You are more likely to meet another hunter. Sportsmen generally tend to be friendly, but I'm sure there are a few grumpy hunters out there. Thankfully, I have never met one.

One sunny mid-February afternoon I was snowshoeing home through several feet of snow. I had been hunting coyote that day, in the heart of a couple of thousand acre forest. The deep snow made it hard to move without snow shoes. I was trying to beat the setting sun as I hustled to the fire lane that would guide me to where I parked my truck. I was a bit upset with myself, not because I had been unable to see any coyotes that day, but because I had inadvertently spooked a yard of deer. At this time of year, with little food and a lot of snow, the deer often bed down close together in the sheltered portions of forest. This is called a "yard". The close proximity helps them conserve energy and protect one another. Often deer gather on the south side of a gentle hill where the sun is strong or in a pine grove where there is some shelter from the wind. While trudging around, I thought I caught site of a whitetail dashing away. As I walked on I found the telltale signs that I had moved a yard of deer. The lima bean shapes in the snow where they had been lying down and the many piles of droppings made it clear. I counted nineteen individual beds. It bothered me to have disturbed them. The coyotes were being trouble enough on top of the weather and lack of food.

While trudging toward the fire lane with my gun on my shoulder, I was upset with myself and not prepared to deal with what came next. As the lane came into view, I saw that it was being travelled by cross-country skier with his dog on a long leash. Normally I would have delayed my emergence from the woods, and stayed still and quiet until he passed by to avoid any encounter. But I wanted to get home and the sun was sinking. So I came out onto the lane about 40 yards ahead of the skier. Covered in blaze orange, a heavy coat, dark glasses, big snow shoes and a long gun glinting in the fiery setting sun, I must have looked a bit intimidating to this fellow. Launching my usual "hunter charm" I tipped my hat and said "hello" before adjusting the rifle, as it began slipping off my shoulder. I rearranged it on the other shoulder and continued to walk onto the lane. The skier yelled: "I'm not a deer! And that there," pointing to his dog, "that isn't a deer either!" My smile disappeared and I stared blankly at the skier, who was now only ten paces from me. "With all due respect, I know darn well you and your dog are not deer." Realizing his mistake, he tried to soften the insult with a smile saying: "Well, you hear all kinds of horror stories about people and their dogs getting shot. You can't be too careful." Doing my best to be polite considering that the insult was not retracted, I continued walking beside him as he skied, remarking how the media enjoys scaring people into thinking that hunters are all dumb and trigger happy.

We actually exchanged names. Scott asked me if it was still deer season as he let his dog Trixie off the leash. Trixie ran ahead quite a distance before slowing down to sniff around in the snow, her black coat creating a stark contrast in the orange glow of the winter sunset. I told him that deer season ended on New Year's Eve and that I was coyote hunting. Surprise to hear that one could hunt coyote, he asked for details. We spoke the whole way back to the parking lot. He was very inquisitive, wanting to know how many deer I had shot that season. I returned the personal interest in my hobby with interest in his. I admitted that my cross-country skis were somewhere in my attic and that seeing him made me think I should take them out and dust them off.

As we approached the last 100 yard stretch of fire lane to the parking lot, we could see Trixie sniffing around near the cars, looking to leave her mark where the other dogs had. Scott asked me how I could get close to the coyotes to get a shot at them. I shared a variety of techniques and mentioned a squeaker that I had in my pocket. He stood amazed. "You mean to tell me that a squeaky sound will call in a coyote?" Taking out the squeaker I stopped walking and said, "Check this out." Scott stared at the little sound maker in my hand. I gave it a squeeze. "SqwEEEEEEeeeek". Trixie, still a hundred yards down the fire lane, stopped instantly and cocked her head, lifting her little floppy ears as high as she could. Her eyes stared straight back to where Scott and I were looking on. I squeaked again and she bolted straight back to us with a mixed look of glee and determination! "You have got to be kidding. That really works!" laughed Scott. I laughed too remarking, "I wish it had worked on the wild dogs earlier today!" We laughed together and patted Trixie who continued to sniff and examine us carefully, still wondering where the squeaky noise had come from. We joked that she deserved a doggie treat for such a great response. By the end of the walk Scott was asking how to get his hunting license. Connecting a friendly face to hunting is important. Be sure to be the friendly face. I'm glad my attitude improved quickly enough during this exchange. As much as it depends on me, I try to be at peace with all people.

There may be occasions when you will want to access a piece of private land. This always requires permission from the land owner. Suppose you discovered beautiful farmland frequented by many deer. Or you found a thirty-acre deer oasis that is completely surrounded by homes, and you can't access it unless you pass through someone's property. It is time to get permission to hunt or pass through land. How should a good hunter approach the land owner? First, remember who you are. You are a guest who is asking for something that nobody is obligated to give to you. You are requesting a favor. Approach the land owner meekly, and consider him or her better than yourself. It may be tempting to begin by talking about getting the deer away from his fruit trees or shrubs, but don't start by offering to solve his wildlife problems as if you're a traveling salesman. Candidly let the owner know that you want to hunt the deer that pass through the land and that you need his permission to do so. As the conversation develops, you can eventually speak about the mutual benefits of an agreement but never start there. People prefer to be humbly asked for help rather than to be offered a deal.

Now I'm really going to sound like your mom. You never get a second chance to make a good first impression. Wash up and shave before you approach a land owner. If you are a woman, I am sure you know how to make yourself look put together. We guys need a bit more coaching in this area. Get cleaned up men. Put on some casual business clothing such as khaki pants and a shirt with a collar. When you ring the doorbell, stand up straight and smile. Impressions matter, especially when the land owner is being approached by a perfect stranger who wants access to his property while carrying a weapon. Appear very responsible. Be confident and have self-respect. You are a good hunter. Identify yourself with your full name and address. Let the owner know that you noticed the deer and that the land was good for hunting. If he allows you access, ask him for the best way to contact him so you can let him know when you will be in the area. Offer your phone number as well. Be sure to send him a thank you card before you start hunting, and at the end of the season send a second thank you card describing the results of your hunt. If you feel generous and it seems appropriate, offer him some meat. Good relationships like these have helped me take home many deer. I presently have permission to hunt on one farm and to pass through one back yard. Everyone involved is happy!

# 17

# One Last Story
## (One Must End With A Success Story)

*I*t was a glorious morning. I was in a new tree stand location before light and the stars were brilliant in the clear sky. As uplifted as the weather made me feel, I was uneasy about my bow shooting ability that morning. I had been practicing with a new bow for the last couple of days and it was performing superbly on my foam target. I purchased the bow in January right after the last hunting season. Despite my stellar practice results, I still had an issue that needed sorting out. Taking shots from as far as 40 yards away had resulted in a consistent grouping of the arrows and had convinced me that I was going to be accurate at 30 yards or less in a real hunting scenario. But I was wrong. I had been in a different tree stand a week before this day's hunt, and I was absolutely stunned when what should have been an easy 15-yard shot on a small buck resulted in a complete miss. I chalked it up to a fluke since my practice sessions had been going so well. Then when another shot taken during a subsequent hunt didn't hit I was so upset that I was sick to my stomach. My confidence in my shooting ability was shaken to the core. I was ready to hang up the new bow and go back to my older bow, and I began to regret having spent so much money on the advanced model with the latest technology. The bow was just not shooting well when it mattered most. Could I blame the bow really? The real question I needed to answer was: "What was I doing differently in the stand than on the ground with the practice target?" I had no answer at the time. To this day I am not absolutely sure what had gone wrong, but eventually I formed a theory. I believe that the new bow design was more sensitive to trigger control mistakes than my first bow. And when I was practicing I was making sure to press the trigger slowly with a classic surprise release of the arrow. But with a living deer in the sights, I may have been jerking the trigger. Unfortunately, sitting in the tree that morning with the new bow, I did not know what was going wrong.

With my previous failures weighing on my mind, I sat in this new tree stand location from which I had not hunted all season. The rut was in full swing so I put a couple of doe estrus scent lures near a mock scrape that I had created. The scrape was not showing much evidence of deer traffic, but there was enough evidence of deer in the general area so I expected to see some action. I could not even bring myself to go and hunt my first choice spot where I had trouble earlier on. Although I am not superstitious, I needed to change my setup and environment just to make me feel better. Nervous but happy, I was hoping to see a deer—but also hoping that I would not have to take a shot. What a crazy mix of emotions. As the light began to come up, I stood and pretended to get ready for a shot. It was a practice move. I wanted to rise slowly and get into a shooting stance without too much movement or noise. And so I did. The air was still and the forest was quiet.

I sat back down and watched as the light began to get stronger. The birds had not started their morning songs, and not even a rodent moved. Then I heard some leaves rustling a long way off behind me. I listened intently, slowly turning my head to look over my right shoulder. I saw nothing. A few seconds passed and the unmistakable sound of a twig snap broke the silence, followed by the sound of hooves on dry leaves. And they were moving at a walking speed! I slowly shifted my weight over my feet and began to stand again rotating toward the sound as I rose. I moved faster than I had just practiced moments ago inspired by the rapid sound of the approaching deer. On my feet and fully turned so the tree was in front of me, I looked for movement. Emerging from the brush came three does, seemingly excited by the scent they detected. They wanted to see who the new doe was. I chuckled silently at the thought. Then the hunting response took over. My respiration increased, and I felt my pulse rise with the anticipation of the encounter. The lead doe passed to the right of the tree straight through my line of fire. She moved too quickly for me to even draw on her. The other two does trotted to the left of the tree passing behind me. I adjusted my feet, keeping my movements in time with their noise and speed. They settled thirty yards beyond my scent wicks, seemingly confused about why the scent was so strong yet no new deer was present. I raised the bow, but did not draw. The threesome stood motionless. Tilting their heads up to catch more scent, they stood silently looking about. After my failures from the week before, I just watched unwilling to draw the bow. The smaller deer began to browse a bit on the wild blueberry bushes. Minutes passed. The weight of past failure was on my mind. I still couldn't bring myself to call or draw or do anything. I just stared as these magnificent creatures with their big, shiny round eyes and moist noses facing in my general direction. Their coats were perfect. The white patches under their necks looked so clean. Had these deer just taken baths? Their weight was good. Their bodies were well-proportioned and healthy. What beautiful specimens.

Then, as though haunted by a phantom, they all startled and stared in the direction from which they had come. For a moment, all three were locked onto something behind my tree. I dared not move because they were looking just below me. Whatever it was, they didn't like it. I stood perfectly still. Then they bolted away. They flew up the hillside beyond me and disappeared. I could not hear or see what spooked them, so I avoided making any sudden moves in case it was something interesting like a coyote or big buck. There I was, motionless with my bow facing the spot where the does had stood, and hearing nothing but a gentle early morning breeze.

A minute past. Then another. Finally I decided to sit back down. My arms were tired and nothing else seemed to be happening. As

I began to relax I caught sight of an antler in the periphery of my vision. It was a big-bodied, five point buck with a nice white set of antlers. Now I knew what spooked the does. I was amazed at how he got so close without my ears detecting him. The buck had his nose up and periodically put it down to the ground as he cautiously moved toward my scent wicks. Because I was already frozen in position, my bow still pointing toward the scent source, I didn't have to re-adjust my stance a bit for a clear shot. I was silently singing in my heart as the buck stopped and scanned the whole area carefully. He even looked up at the tree stand and back down again without noticing me. He was fooled. I drew the bow very slowly, painstakingly, not wanting to display any movement. As I passed through the peak of the bow's draw weight, my arm muscles began to quiver. My brain gave no heed to my complaining muscles, commanding my arms to hold the draw and steady the bow while my eye put the sight picture together. He passed in front of me at 15 yards. My throat readied a grunt to make him stop at just the right moment so I could rest the dot on his heart. My mind suppressed all thoughts of failure. The red dot jittered over his side, unable to settle on his moving form. The command went to my throat to grunt the deer-like guttural sound in the hope that he would pause to listen. Even if the buck stopped for just a second, it would be long enough to settle the sights and launch the arrow for the short flight to his heart. My mouth opened in response to the plan and air blew through my larynx. But no sound came out. Nothing. My bow arm shook as if in disbelief of my vocal failure. It wanted to say, "Hey, I'm doing my part here and hurting all the while. All you have to do this morning is GRUNT!" The buck walked on and the shot opportunity passed. He turned right and walked straight away, my sights resting on his tail and haunches. I slowly lowered the bow to my leg, keeping the full draw but easing the tension on my left arm. The buck continued to turn right. I swallowed hard, hoping my throat would be useful should I need it. He kept on his curved path, seeking the source of the scent. Suddenly he stopped thirty yards away from me in a great location. His head was behind a tree that blocked his view of me. The rest of his body was exposed, giving me clear broadside access to his vitals. I prepared to shoot.

Just when things could not look any better, panic struck me. A voice spoke in my head, "You couldn't make the closer shots last week. You have no business taking a chance and wounding this animal." I prayed for guidance. Raising the bow, I set the dot on the inside of the front leg. I slid the dot up the foreleg and over the body. It came to rest just behind the shoulder and a bit below the center. The dot shook, then settled. My breath was held and I began to apply pressure to the trigger, but not much. Seconds passed. The deer didn't move. I prayed that God would fly the arrow. I applied slightly more pressure to the trigger, but I could not bring myself to press any harder. The deer remained still. Was I crazy? This scenario could not be any better! The ideal shot at a handsome buck was pending for an unusually long time, yet I could not let the darn arrow fly. Insanity! Coming to my senses, I realized just how fabulous the situation was and how all the preparation and effort had culminated in this very moment. I was being given a shot that was too good to be true, and it was not going away even though I was stalling. I would kick myself if I did not try. I slowly pressed the trigger through the sheer point and watched as the arrow flew straight through the air and disappeared right into the spot where my sight rested. It passed through both lungs and struck the heart. Perfect shot!

The buck bolted up the hill almost in line with where the does had gone. I marveled that he did not instantly appear impacted by the fatal wound. He was running hard and bounding away for a few seconds. At full speed he covered at least 70 yards. Then he began to circle to the right almost turning back toward me. The circle got tighter and he fell dead, facing my direction. It was a clean kill. The arrow was sticking out of the earth with the fletching pointing straight at me like a lone flower on the leaf-covered floor. I was overcome with a rush of joy and relief — almost to the point of tears.

No tracking was required for this buck. After giving thanks and calling my wife, I climbed down from the tree, my hands shaking almost uncontrollably from the leftover adrenaline. I walked over and pulled the arrow out of the ground. It took extraordinary self-discipline to examine that arrow and follow my deer recovery procedure. All I wanted to do was to run across the forest "hootin and hollerin!" With the spent arrow returned to my quiver, I tracked the buck to where he rested even though I didn't need to. This exercise gave me additional tracking practice and helped me calm down. After tagging the deer, I began dragging it home. Within minutes I had it on my lawn behind my house. My lovely wife was already waiting in the driveway with the camera.

This exciting hunt and most of the other ones I have shared with you all occurred within a quarter mile of quiet residential neighborhoods. Some were within shouting distance from my back door. Only the elk hunt and the bear hunt references occurred in deeper wilderness areas. So what is the difference between hunting the deep wilderness and the smaller neighborhood or town forests? Not much. You must be more certain of your target and what is behind it when hunting near residential areas. And with a little care that certainty is very achievable as you enjoy the benefits of local woodlands: the brief gas-saving commute to your hunting spot, the peace of mind of knowing you are within reliable radio and cellular range if you ever need emergency assistance or a friend to help you drag your big buck to your truck. Trust me; you can experience the great thrills of the hunt in a "forgotten wilderness" as close to home as minutes down the road or a half hour's drive. Some of you will be able to access hunting grounds just a short walk from your back door as I do. Whether you hunt whitetail in the deep forests far from civilization or become a backyard sportsman like me, I hope that you reap all the rewards of your efforts and gain an intimate connection with the land and the herd. I've given you the tools to get started no matter where you hunt, and I believe you will enjoy a mutually beneficial experience when you give to and take from nature as God has intended. So get out there and put your heart into hunting. I wish you the best!

The buck bagged with the new bow

# Appendix

# A Basic Hunter's Day Pack

- 16oz of water, plastic sandwich bag filled with nuts, raisins, fruit or a peanut butter sandwich
- A small roll of toilet paper to be used as a disposable trail marker or for other personal needs
- Night time reflective trail markers, blaze orange tape
- Headlamp, LED type and spare batteries
- Compass, compact GPS, topographical map
- Compact bow saw, fixed blade knife if you do not keep it on your person
- Rubber or Latex gloves
- Copy of hunting license and firearm license in a plastic sandwich bag to keep it dry
- Two ball point pens (not flare pens – they freeze), two elastic bands
- Survival blanket, waterproof matches, tinder, signal mirror
- 12 feet of 5/8inch nylon rope for dragging the deer or other contingencies

- Scent bottles
- Cellular phone or radio
- Miniature first aid kit
- Binoculars
- Broad head wrench, spare ammunition
- Hand warmers

CPSIA information can be obtained at www.ICGtesting.com
Printed in the USA
BVOW032325020513

319743BV00002B/94/P